Number Theory for Elementary School Teachers

Number Theory for Elementary School Teachers

Edward S. Wall

The City College of New York

 **Higher Education**

Boston   Burr Ridge, IL   Dubuque, IA   New York
San Francisco   St. Louis   Bangkok   Bogotá   Caracas   Kuala Lumpur
Lisbon   London   Madrid   Mexico City   Milan   Montreal   New Delhi
Santiago   Seoul   Singapore   Sydney   Taipei   Toronto

Higher Education

This book is printed on acid-free paper.

1 2 3 4 5 6 7 8 9 0 FGR/FGR 0 9

ISBN: 978-0-07-337847-3
MHID: 0-07-337847-X

Editor in Chief: *Michael Ryan*
Editorial Director: *Beth Mejia*
Publisher: *David Patterson*
Sponsoring Editor: *Allison McNamara*
Editorial Coordinator: *Sarah Kiefer*
Developmental Editor: *Jill Eccher*
Marketing Manager: *James Headley*
Project Manager: *Rachel J. Castillo*
Cover Designer: *Mary-Presley Adams*
Design Manager: *Ashley Bedell*
Production Supervisor: *Tandra Jorgensen*
Composition: *Macmillan Publishing Solutions*
Printing: *45# New Era Matte Plus, Quebecor World, Inc.*

Library of Congress Cataloging-in-Publication Data

Wall, Edward.
 Number theory for elementary school teachers / Edward Wall. —1st ed.
   p. cm.
 Includes index.
 ISBN-13: 978-0-07-337847-3 (alk. paper)
 ISBN-10: 0-07-337847-X (alk. paper)
 1. Number theory. 2. Elementary school teachers—Training of. 3. Elementary school teachers—In-service training. I. Title.
 QA241.W325 2010
 512.7—dc22

                                                    2008049014

About *The Practical Guide Series*

New teachers face a seemingly endless set of challenges—classroom management, assessment, motivation, content knowledge, cultural responsiveness, inclusion, technology—just to name a few. Preparing for the profession can at times seem overwhelming. Teacher candidates may begin to see solutions to some of the anticipated challenges as they progress through a program of study but know that there are many that await them in their first classroom. Support by mentors and colleagues is crucial for beginning teachers, and this series is designed to bolster that guidance. *The Practical Guide Series* provides another level of support for these new and future professionals.

The series was conceived in response to concerns about teacher retention, especially among teachers in their first to fourth years in the classroom when mentorship and guidance play a crucial role. These titles offer future and beginning teachers a collection of practical advice that they can refer to in student teaching and in the early teaching years. Instructors of pre-service teachers can use these books to reinforce concepts in their texts with additional applications, use them to foster discussion, and help guide pre-service students in their practice teaching.

Besides addressing issues of basic concern to new teachers, we anticipate generating a level of excitement—one that a traditional textbook is hard-pressed to engender—that will further motivate entrants into this most essential profession with a contagious enthusiasm. A positive start to a teaching career is the best path to becoming a master teacher!

Alfred S. Posamentier, *Series Editor*
Dean, The School of Education,
The City College of New York

To Malcolm Dade Wall, as I promised

Contents

Preface xi

INTRODUCTION xiii

Numbers in the Everyday World xiv

Numbers in the Classroom xiv

Number Theory xvi

CHAPTER 1   *Mathematical Explanations and Arguments 1*

Reasoning and Proof from a Historical Perspective 2

Reasoning and Proof from a Developmental Perspective 3

Varieties of Proof 3

CHAPTER 2   *Counting and Recording of Numbers 11*

Numbers and Counting from a Historical Perspective 11

Numbers and Counting from a Developmental Perspective 14

The Art of Counting 15

Positional Number Systems 21

Large Numbers 23

CHAPTER 3   *Sums 26*

Addition from a Historical Perspective 26

Addition from a Developmental Perspective 29

Whole-Number Addition Algorithms 32

Arithmetic Series and Figurate Numbers 37

Indeterminate Problems 41

CHAPTER 4   *Differences 46*

Subtraction from a Historical Perspective 46

Subtraction from a Developmental Perspective 49

Whole-Number Subtraction Algorithms 52

Negative Numbers 57

CHAPTER 5   *Multiples 65*

Multiplication from a Historical Perspective 65

Multiplication from a Developmental Perspective 70

Whole-Number Multiplication Algorithms 72

Prime Numbers and Factoring 75

CHAPTER 6   *Divisibility and Remainders 81*

Division from a Historical Perspective 81

Division from a Developmental Perspective 85

Whole-Number Division Algorithms 87

Clock and Modular Arithmetic 90

Divisibility Rules 94

Casting Out Nines 95

Indeterminate Problems Yet Again 96

CHAPTER 7   *Fractions 100*

Fractions from a Historical Perspective 100

Fractions from a Developmental
      Perspective 102

Fraction Arithmetic 103

Ratios and Proportionality 114

CHAPTER 8   *Decimals 119*

Decimals from a Historical Perspective 119

Decimals from a Developmental
      Perspective 120

Decimal Arithmetic 122

Nonterminating Decimals 125

CHAPTER 9   *Real Numbers 129*

The Reals from a Historical Perspective 131

The Reals from a Developmental
      Perspective 135

Arithmetic with the Reals 136

Pythagorean Theorem 139

Continued Fractions 143

CHAPTER 10   *Transfinite Numbers 147*

Infinity from a Historical Perspective 147

Infinity from a Developmental
      Perspective 149

Varieties of Infinity 151

Arithmetic with Infinite Numbers 156

APPENDIX   *Tools for Understanding 161*

Variables 161

Subscripts and Exponents 162

Fundamental Properties of Arithmetic 162

Fundamental Theorem of Arithmetic 163

Index 166

Preface

This text was written to fill a void that seems to exist in the standard mathematics and mathematics education curriculum for elementary pre-service teachers. Specifically, I see a hiatus between mathematics courses that focus on extending pre-service teachers' fluency with and deepening their understanding of *the mathematics* of the preK–6 curriculum, and mathematics education courses that focus on extending pre-service teachers' fluency with and deepening their understanding of *ways of teaching mathematics* in the preK–6 grades. At present, whatever is learned seems to be ineffectively reiterated across the pre-service curriculum. Pre-service teachers receive a background in mathematics isolated from the realities of children's learning of mathematics, and they receive a background in children's learning of mathematics isolated from the realities of the structure of the mathematics being learned.

This hiatus might be bridged by taking seriously the notion of integrating content knowledge and knowledge about teaching mathematics. For instance, it might be possible to blend, within pre-service curricular experiences, substantial knowledge of mathematics and substantial knowledge about the developmental aspects of children's learning of mathematics. This text can be envisioned as a step in that direction. It has been modeled somewhat on certain of the undergraduate number theory texts of the 1940s (for example, that of Oystein Ore[1]) in that the subject matter is similar and there are reasonably well-developed historical references. The primary difference is that in this text, the reasons for taking up a particular topic are tied concretely—often through short vignettes—to the mathematical work and thinking that children are doing in classrooms. Thus the text directly addresses much of the mathematics of preK–6 and does it in a manner that both provides relevant and pragmatic motivations for looking deeper into preK–6 mathematics and gives the reader some insight into its deeper structure.

This is not a text to be merely read. It is meant to be worked. Mathematical ideas are not matters for superficial recitation. Rather, they are meant to be engaged and explored; they are meant to be understood in the doing. Often the doing of mathematics becomes somewhat like hastening through a beautiful park just because it is a shortcut to our destination. Unlike the ambling child, we seldom tarry to examine a special flower or impulsively stroll down a circuitous detour. We do save time, but our experience is impoverished.

---

[1] Oystein Ore, *Number Theory and Its History* (New York: McGraw-Hill, 1948).

Thus—and here I paraphrase Deborah Loewenberg Ball[2]—I have written this text partly to open the eyes of teachers and pre-service teachers to the awesome mathematical capabilities of the children they teach—children who most often assimilate, in just a few years, mathematics that it took smart men and women centuries to grasp. Bearing in mind the exuberance that children often bring to mathematics,[3] I have also written this text to give these selfsame teachers added pleasure in their own doing of mathematics. Perhaps this will be among the texts that will "open up mathematics to [service and pre-service teachers] in the ways they need and deserve."[4] Perhaps, as I attempt, in my own teaching of mathematics methods, to "open doors to . . . students' learning of mathematics,"[5] this text will lead my own students beyond my attempts—a pleasure that is at the very core of the educative process.

✄ Acknowledgments

I wish to thank, among others, Deborah Loewenberg Ball, who made this book probable, and Alfred S. Posamentier, who made it possible.

Edward S. Wall
The City College of New York

[2] Deborah Loewenberg Ball, The Permutations Project: Mathematics as a context for learning and teaching. In *Exploring Teaching: Reinventing an Introductory Course,* ed. S. Feinman-Nemser and H. Featherstone (New York: Teachers College Press, 1992).
[3] E. A. Silver, M. E. Strutchens, and J. S. Zawojewski. NAEP findings regarding race/ethnicity and gender: Affective issues, mathematics performance, and instructional context. In *Results from the Sixth Mathematics Assessment of the National Assessment of Educational Progress,* ed. P. A. Kenney and E. A. Silver (Reston, VA: National Council of Teachers of Mathematics, 1997), pp. 33–59.
[4] Ball, The Permutations Project, p. 30.
[5] Ball, The Permutations Project, p. 30.

Introduction

The art of arithmetic, it would seem, is part of our genetic heritage. Babies, in their sixth month, show an ability to recognize small numbers of objects—two to three—and to "combine them in elementary additions and subtractions."[1] Such dispositions (as in the raising of three fingers to indicate a third birthday) carry through early childhood into the primary grades. But unfortunately, and for reasons that are not yet fully understood, interest and curiosity are often replaced by frustration and boredom by the upper elementary grades.

Simultaneously, a child's everyday taking up of arithmetic is driven, as it has been throughout recorded history, by the marketplace. It is there in coinage, in the purchasing of food, in how one weighs a pound, and in how one measures an inch. Such influences may be even more powerful than those experienced in school. Consider the following vignette.[2]

> Peter is a second grader and is quite proficient in the writing, counting, and addition of numbers. His mother's birthday is coming up, and he wishes to buy her a present that has a price tag of 25 cents. He puts aside his allowance, and on the fateful day he enters the store, marches up to the proprietor, points to the item in question, and carefully places his coins—two pennies and a nickel—on the counter.

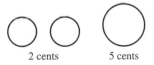

2 cents   5 cents

> The proprietor looks at the amount and says, "That's only seven cents. This costs twenty-five cents."

At this moment, Peter confronts place value. His dutiful and skillful performance of second grade mathematics is tempered in the necessities of the mathematics of the marketplace. Peter, I suggest, is not atypical.

---

[1] Stanislas Dehane, *The Number Sense* (New York: Oxford University Press, 1997), p. 62.
[2] This vignette dates to the 1950s.

✖ Numbers in the Everyday World

School, it has been said, exists largely for the purpose of socializing children and, with an eye to adult life, inculcating crucial skills, such as reading, writing, and arithmetic. Although it is clear that a lack of skill in arithmetic raises barriers to the pursuit of many careers, it is not so clear what the tradeoff is between mastery of school arithmetic and adult success in the marketplace. The mathematics educator Marilyn Burns writes of a conversation with a friend, Barbara, who is an accomplished interior decorator:

> "I was never good at math," she once told me. "I'm so grateful that I have work to do that doesn't rely on doing math."
>
> I looked at her in amazement. To do her work, she has to measure the dimensions of rooms for floor covering and wallpaper, figure yardage for drapes and upholstery, calculate the cost of the goods, and prepare invoices for clients, figuring in the percentage for her services. I've watched Barbara size up rooms, her eyes darting as she takes in the floor area, the ceiling height, the placement of windows and doors; suggest the right amount, size and scale of furniture; prepare an estimate that is amazingly close to actual cost. I experienced this firsthand when we remodeled our house. No math? What was she talking about?
>
> I asked her. "'Oh that,' she said, "That's easy. It's those pages of math problems in the book I never could do."[3]

The mathematics of Barbara and Peter is the mathematics of the everyday world, so it is often learned through a degree of trial and error. This is typical of such mathematics and was typical of most doing of mathematics—with the notable exception, in the West, of a brief period of Greek history—until about the thirteenth century.[4] What I find of interest in all this is that Peter's everyday mathematics experience, in a sense, brings understanding to his school experience. And Barbara's everyday mathematics experience, though it seems to have little relationship to those remembered pages in her math text, brings understanding to her chosen profession. Both Barbara and Peter appear to be at a point where they have acquired, in their own ways, a deeper understanding of their own using of mathematics. They have, or are developing, computational fluency.

✖ Numbers in the Classroom

I don't wish to give the impression that the mathematics of the classroom has nothing to do with the mathematics of the marketplace. Of course, it has much in common with the mathematics of the everyday. Nonetheless, it is unclear how the mathematics of the classroom transfers across the boundaries of school.[5] This lack suggests to some that teachers should exert substantial effort in trying to contextualize mathematics, trying to make it *realistic* and hence *relevant*. This,

---

[3] Marilyn Burns, *Math: Facing an American Phobia* (Sausalito, CA: Math Solutions, 1998).
[4] See, for example, Jens Høyrup, *In Measure, Number, and Weight* (Albany: SUNY, 1994).
[5] See, for example, Jean Lave, *Cognition in Practice* (New York: Cambridge University Press, 1988).

however, may be a trap. The school context itself is somewhat artificial and, perhaps necessarily, provides relatively few *realistic* life experiences. Children are not necessarily being directly equipped by their school experience to engage in interior decorating, to farm, to sell candy or produce, to tailor clothing, or to place a pixel on a computer screen. They are instead being broadly prepared to take responsible positions in a highly technological society. They are, one hopes, being prepared to be thoughtfully and creatively critical. Exactly what this might look like is still unclear. However, let's start by considering the following vignette.

> It is a moderately typical day in a moderately typical classroom with moderately typical students. However, it wasn't. My students began with a series of simple questions that left me gasping for answers.
>
> "Mr. Smith, where do numbers come from? Who invented zero?"
> "They come from the past," I mumbled, barely concealing my ignorance.
> "Can you tell us how the Romans did their arithmetic?" another asked. "I've been trying to do multiplication with Roman numerals for days, and I'm getting nowhere with it."
> "You can't do arithmetic with those numerals," another student interrupts.
> "My dad told me the Romans did arithmetic like the Chinese do today, with an abacus."[6]

What does one do in a case like this?

An answer that respectfully takes into account such student questions needs to reflect a school mathematics that goes beyond rote procedural learning[7] and includes a significant amount of conceptual understanding. How a teacher is to frame all this, in today's postmodern era, has recently provoked contentious debate. Nonetheless, two things stand out. First, most young children[8] come to our classrooms with immense mathematical talent. That talent, as the students in this vignette demonstrate, is grounded both in mathematics conversations with parents and peers and in their own mathematics experiments.

Nonetheless, we teachers often seem to pay little mind to what children are thinking. If a child insists that

$$
\begin{array}{r}
200 \\
-190 \\
\hline
190
\end{array}
$$

arguing that 0 from 0 is 0, that you cannot take 9 from 0 so you leave the 9, and that 1 from 1 is 1, then there is indeed a need for remediation. But it may be I, the teacher, whose approach needs to change! Listening with respect, listening even though you ache to speak, encourages receptiveness and productive discussion. Not surprisingly, listening so as to entrap may engender wariness and dislike.

---

[6] Adapted from Georges Ifrah, *The Universal History of Numbers*. Translated from the French by David Bellos, E. F. Harding, Sophie Wood, and Ian Monk (New York: Wiley, 2000).
[7] I suspect there is some misunderstanding about the terms *conceptual* and *procedural*. Being procedurally competent usually includes some conceptual understanding of why and what one is doing.
[8] Although there may be notable exceptions, there are very few.

Second, the ability to listen respectfully to the mathematics of the elementary school child seems to derive from one's own knowledge and appreciation of this mathematics. Mr. Smith seems ignorant of the historical development of mathematics. Rather than seizing the opportunity that his students' questions offer to discuss zero, place value, or the standard multiplication algorithm, Mr. Smith can do little more than *gasp*. Unfortunately, such knowledge and appreciation are rare in mathematicians and elementary school teachers alike. Perhaps that is because, for adults, what was once new and challenging now seems obvious or even tedious. When teaching arithmetic, we seldom speak about the history of working with numbers or the excitement of a profound understanding of fundamental mathematics.[9]

❈ Number Theory

Keeping all this in mind, this book is primarily an exploration of the mathematics of the elementary school classroom. In that sense it is directed inward, to examining the foundations of that mathematics, so that you, the teacher, can reexamine your understanding of this mathematics and the mathematics understandings of your students. I have tried to weave classroom mathematics and the mathematics of the everyday into an informing whole and then to reexamine the principles that give it life. At times, this has led me to detail the structure of a particular algorithm in the context of both what the algorithm entails and the rather awesome mathematics development of children. At other times, it has led me to review the development of such algorithms and their parallels in today's school mathematics curriculum.

Whichever approach I took, I found that the mathematics I addressed was best framed by a theory of number that predates Pythagoras—a theory of number within which number theory and the mathematics of the marketplace are playfully integrated with what has been termed recreational mathematics. Oystein Ore, among others, appears to attest to such connections[10] in his discussion of "Intermediate Problems" as he relates the curious calculation

Houses	7
Cats	49
Mice	343
Ears of wheat	2,401
Hekat measure	16,807
Total	19,607

which appears in the Rhind Papyrus (ca. 1650 BC), to a problem in Leonardo Pisano's *Liber Abaci* (AD 1202):[11]

Seven old women on the road to Rome, each woman has seven mules, each mule carries seven sacks, each sack contains seven loaves, with each loaf there

---

[9] For some discussion of this, see Liping Ma, *Knowing and Teaching Elementary Mathematics* (Mahwah, NJ: Erlbaum, 1999).
[10] *Number Theory and Its History*, pp. 116–117.
[11] A more recent incarnation of this problem involves the meaning of the word *met*. It begins "As I was going to St. Ives, I met a man with seven wives" and ends with the twist "How many were going to St. Ives?"

are seven knives, and each knife is in seven sheaths. How many objects are there, women, mules, sacks, loaves, knives, and sheaths?

Dickson, in this regard, notes that interest in the theory of number is "shared on the one extreme by nearly every noted mathematician and on the other extreme by numerous amateurs attracted by no other part of mathematics."[12]

Recreational mathematics, although it does not necessarily depict life or the real, continues to provide engaging contexts for exploring mathematics. For a century and a quarter, there was the *Ladies' Diary*,[13] whose subtitle declares, "Containing New Improvements in ARTS and SCIENCES, and many entertaining PARTICULARS: Designed for the USE AND DIVERSION OF THE FAIR SEX." There were the mathematical puzzles of Sam Loyd[14] published in the *Brooklyn Daily Eagle* (1890–1911) and in the *Woman's Home Companion* (1904–1911). There was Martin Gardner's *Scientific American* column "Mathematical Games," which ran from 1956 through 1986. And today there are certain of the weekly puzzlers aired on National Public Radio's "Car Talk":[15]

> Recently I had a visit with my mom and we realized that the two digits that make up my age, when reversed, resulted in her age. For example, if she's 73, I'm 37. We wondered how often this has happened over the years, but we got sidetracked with other topics and we never came up with an answer.
>
> When I got home, I figured out that the digits of our ages have been reversible six times so far. I also figured out that if we're lucky it would happen again in a few years, and if we're really lucky it would happen one more time after that. In other words, it would have happened 8 times over all. So the question is, how old am I now?

That such mathematics is part of our everyday experience is not inconsequential. The mathematician Richard Guy is reputed[16] to have said, "The bulk of mathematics has really always been recreational. . . . Only a tiny fraction of all mathematics is actually applied or used."

Such orientation as this means that, depending on the reader, I may have touched on previously unexplored mathematics vistas in order to suggest the depths and delights in what might seem the mathematically mundane. I have tried to keep the manipulation of symbols to a minimum—the Appendix may help with interpreting those that do appear—but symbols are an essential part of the doing of mathematics as it has evolved, for efficiency's sake, to become heavily graphical.

[12] Leonard Eugene Dickson, *History of the Theory of Numbers: Divisibility and Primality* (New York: Chelsea, 1952), p. iii.
[13] First published in 1704. Shelly Costa gives an intriguing analysis of the readership in The "Ladies' Diary": Gender, mathematics, and civil society in early-eighteenth-century England. Osiris, 2nd series, Vol. 17, *Science and Civil Society* (2002), pp. 49–73.
[14] See, for instance, Sam Loyd, *Mathematical Puzzles of Sam Loyd*, ed. Martin Gardner (New York: Dover, 1959).
[15] Adapted slightly from a puzzle in the Car Talk archive (http://www.cartalk.com/content/puzzler/transcripts/200813/index.html). Accessed June 15, 2008.
[16] See http://www.maa.org/mathland/mathland_7_14.html. Accessed June 9, 2008.

Mathematical Explanations and Arguments

The focus of this chapter is on the art of mathematical explanations and arguments. First I will examine this art historically and developmentally, and then you and I will take a closer look at some of the more common forms of mathematical argument and explanations that characterize the modern notion of proof. My purpose here is not to teach proof—although I will ask, here and in later chapters, that you attempt a proof—but to provide a modest introduction to the skills of doing and reading proofs.

To set the stage, so to speak, let's begin with a short vignette from a kindergarten classroom. Ms. Austin-Page has been using unit blocks to help her kindergartners extend and develop their sense of space. In this vignette,[1] we listen as Ms. Austin-Page asks the class what they have learned today.

> Jose waves his hand frantically, exclaiming, "I can prove that a triangle equals a square." Ms. Austin-Page asks him to tell the class more about his discovery, and Jose goes to the block corner and returns with two half-unit (square) blocks, two half-unit (triangle) blocks, and one unit (rectangle) block.

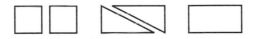

> "See," he says proudly. "If these two [he holds up the square half-units] are the same as this one [he holds up the rectangular unit],

> and these two [he now holds up the triangular half-units] are the same as this one (he holds up the rectangular unit again)

[1]Adapted from A. G. Andrews. Solving geometric problems by using unit blocks. *Teaching Children Mathematics*, 6 (1999), 318–323.

then this square has to be the same as this triangle [he holds up the square half-unit and the triangle half-unit]!"

Although Jose's wording—his assertion that the shapes were "equal"—was not mathematically correct (the shapes are not, for example, congruent), I find myself intrigued by his explanation and his use of the term *proof*. What if, for example, he had said, "The area of this square equals the area of this triangle because each of them is half the area of the same larger rectangle" and then proceeded in his demonstration? In what sense might this be considered a proof or, at least, a compelling demonstration?

⚔ Reasoning and Proof from a Historical Perspective

The history of mathematical explanations and arguments is complicated by the fact that what we now take as paradigmatic of mathematical proof is a methodology that arose around 300 BC, largely thanks to the efforts of Euclid of Alexandria. Nonetheless, as Figure 1.1 indicates,[2] the civilizations of both India and China produced much in the way of mathematical explanations and arguments that Euclid, quite possibly, later codified in his *Elements*. One example is their statement of and solutions for what has come to be known as the Pythagorean *theorem* (that the sum of the squares of the two sides of a right triangle is equal to the square of the third side).

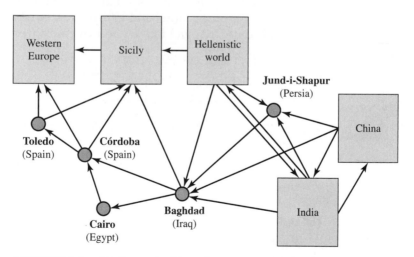

FIGURE 1.1   *Mathematical Development during the Dark Ages*

[2]Slightly adapted from George Gheverghese Joseph, *The Crest of the Peacock: Non-European Roots of Mathematics* (New York: St. Martin's, 1991), p. 10.

In the light of Euclid's *Elements*, these earlier arguments and explanations should be considered convincing demonstrations.[3] For, as Joseph notes,[4] there is an essential difference between Indian proof (*upapattis*), and Greek proof (*apodeixis*). The aim of an Indian scholar was to convince the intelligent student of validity, so a visual demonstration was an accepted form of argument. The Greek *apodeixis*, on the other hand, though it often included a geometric demonstration, was built on selected axioms and relied on propositional logic. Both, Joseph argues, employed logical deduction.

✖ Reasoning and Proof from a Developmental Perspective

As I have indicated, the notion of proof occurs quite early in development. Jose, our kindergartner, certainly has supplied a compelling demonstration—one that depends on the shape of the blocks, the shape of the squares, and the shape of the produced rectangle. Jose's experiential approach to proof is somewhat typical of what is seen in the elementary school curriculum. I am able to prove that 5 is the solution to

$$3 + ? = 8$$

by trying out the numbers from 1 to 10. There is, in a sense, no need in the early years to employ other than thoughtful trial and error.

Around the third grade there is often a change in the perceived effectiveness of trial and error. The counting skills of children have developed to the point where they have begun to realize that "numbers go on forever." Statements such as

An even number plus an odd number equals an odd number

though demonstrable for numbers of moderate size, are not demonstrable for truly large numbers. Now, children are often asked to believe in the structure of a system that they can no longer evaluate on their fingers.

✖ Varieties of Proof

I'm going to discuss briefly four varieties of proof: proof by exhaustion, postulational proof, proof by induction, and proof by contradiction. These varieties differ in structure, but they have at least three things in common. They require that you, the proof giver, have noticed some kind of systematic pattern (for instance, Jose has noticed that two triangles and two squares make a particular rectangle). They require that you make some kind of claim about the pattern you see. (In the elementary grades this is often called a *conjecture*; however,

---

[3] This is not to downplay their mathematical importance. The number-theoretic work of Diophantus of Alexandria can be seen, in part, as an attempt to systematize the solution to a number of ancient word problems.
[4] Quoted in George Gheverghese Joseph, 1994. Different ways of knowing: Contrasting styles of argument in Indian and Greek mathematical traditions. In *Mathematics, Education and Philosophy: An International Perspective*, ed. Paul Ernest (London: The Falmer Press, 1994), pp. 185–204.

stronger claims include *propositions, lemmas,* or *theorems.*) And they require you defend that claim in a logical manner.

Proof by Exhaustion

Here is a problem[5] that might be posed in a third grade classroom (downsized in a second grade classroom and upsized in fourth grade classroom and beyond):

> I have pennies, nickels, and dimes in my pocket, and I pull out three coins. What would be the different amounts that I could have?

P R O B L E M   1 . 1

Write this problem down on a piece of paper. Close this book and first attempt your own systematic solution.

If you are tempted to skip this step (or to skip any of the problems in this book), remember that mathematics is something you *do*, not something you merely reflect on. In this it is a bit like swimming. It is a bad idea to jump into deep water without first practicing those strokes you have read so much about.

A possible solution (with some teacher help in charting) might take the form shown in Figure 1.2. There are, as you can see, ten solutions to this problem. However, is that all? In fact, can you *prove* there are only ten?

When asked this question, students often respond that they tried a lot of combinations but that after a while, the combinations began repeating. Others say that they and their classmates have the same number of solutions, so that must be all. This type of response may be somewhat convincing, but it is not a

Pennies	Nickels	Dimes	Total
1	1	1	16¢
	3		15¢
1		2	21¢
2	1		7¢
2		1	12¢
		3	30¢
1	2		11¢
	2	1	20¢
	1	2	25¢
3			3¢

FIGURE 1.2   *First Solution for Three Coins*

---

[5]Devised by Deborah Loewenberg Ball.

Pennies	Nickels	Dimes	Total
3			3¢
2	1		7¢
1	2		11¢
	3		15¢
2		1	12¢
1	1	1	16¢
	2	1	20¢
1		2	21¢
	1	2	25¢
		3	30¢

FIGURE 1.3   *Second Solution for Three Coins*

proof. I need some sort of patterned presentation that will provide the basis for a convincing argument. How about Figure 1.3 ?

I note in reference to this second solution that the alternatives are that I have no dimes, one dime, two dimes, or three dimes. So I have four cases:

1. *No dimes.* Well, I have at most three pennies. So starting with those three pennies, I exchange, step-by-step, each penny for a nickel. I get exactly four combinations.
2. *One dime.* Well, I have at most two pennies. So starting with those two pennies, I exchange, step-by-step, each penny for a nickel. I get exactly three combinations.
3. *Two dimes.* Well, I have at most one penny. So starting with that one penny, I exchange, step-by-step, each penny for a nickel. I get exactly two combinations.
4. *Three dimes.* That is just one combination.

Thus—and this is a typical proof by exhaustion—there are exactly ten solutions to the problem.

Note that thanks to the patterning, there is a sense in which my second solution is more aesthetically pleasing than my first. Further, note that I don't need to specify combinations, because the solution to the problem can be obtained as follows: Begin with the smallest amount—pennies alone—and then, to that 3¢,

1. Add 4¢ a total of three times (7¢, 11¢, 15¢).
2. Add 9¢ for a total of 12¢, and to that 12¢ add 4¢ a total of two times (16¢ and 20¢).
3. Add 18¢ (9¢ + 9¢) for a total of 21¢, and to that 21¢ add 4¢ for a total of one time (25¢).
4. Add 27¢ (9¢ + 9¢ + 9¢) for a total of 30¢.

Thus the total number of solutions is 4 + 3 + 2 + 1 = 10.

P R O B L E M   1 . 2

a. In my solution, explain where the 4¢ and 9¢ come from.

b. Prove that for 4 coins the solutions are: 4¢, 8¢, 12¢, 16¢, 20¢, 13¢, 17¢, 21¢, 25¢, 22¢, 26¢, 30¢, 31¢, 35¢, 40¢ and, of course, the number of solutions is exactly $5 + 4 + 3 + 2 + 1 = 15$.

Postulational Proofs

Such proofs—proofs by *apodeixis*—tend to be far more efficient than proofs by exhaustion because they usually build on axioms, definitions, and some observed patterning. If, for example, I wanted to extend the coin problem to larger and larger numbers of coins, then a proof by exhaustion would indeed become exhausting. Whereas the coin problem does lend itself to *apodeixis*, I will here give two postulational proofs of

> An even number plus an even number equals an even number

The first I have observed in third grade classrooms; the second is more typical in a beginning algebra course.

In giving a postulational proof, I need to move logically from some known facts—most often definitions and/or axioms—to some new fact. In the third grade, the usual definition for *even number* is that it is the count of a group of objects every one of which has a partner. For example,

$2 = 1+1$ $10 = (1+1) + (1+1) + (1+1) + (1+1) + (1+1)$

A third grade postulational proof goes roughly as follows:

> A number is even if and only if it is a group of pairs. Adding two even numbers is the same as combining the two groups of pairs. But then you have a group of pairs that, by definition, represents an even number.

Here's a symbolic postulational proof. Again I need a definition of *even number*. A beginning algebra student might say a number is even if and only if it is of the form $2 \cdot n$, where n is a whole number. The proof goes roughly as follows:

> You have two even numbers, $2 \cdot n$ and $2 \cdot m$, where m and n are whole numbers. Their sum is

$$2 \cdot n + 2 \cdot m = 2 \cdot (m + n)$$

> However, because $m + n$ is a whole number,[6] I have, by definition, $2 \cdot (m + n)$ is an even number.

---

[6] An important and legitimate mathematical question is "How do I know that $m + n$ is indeed a whole number?" I have, as I indicated I might in the introduction, assumed this fact for the purpose of presentation. However, you may wish to look deeper.

P R O B L E M   1 . 3

Prove that an even number plus an odd number equals an odd number. *Hint:* You have a definition for an even number. You need a definition for an odd number.

Proofs by Induction

The line between mathematical induction and postulational proof blurs a bit,
because mathematical induction requires apodictic reasoning (reasoning based
on the Greek proof, *apodeixis*). However, induction proofs take a special form,
and they are especially effective when we wish to establish a statement that is
true for all whole numbers. Therefore, it is well worth singling out these proofs
in a section of their own. The idea is as follows:

1. I demonstrate that the first statement P_0 in an infinite sequence of state-
    ments is true (it is not necessary to start with 0, by the way).
2. I then prove (effectively a postulational proof) that if arbitrary
    statement P_n in the infinite sequence of statements is true, as are all
    the statements preceding that arbitrary statement, then so is the next
    statement P_{n+1}.

If I can do this, then since my choice of the statement P_n was arbitrary, it must
be true for all statements. Think about it. Say there was a first statement P_{m+1} in
my sequence that was false. Thus, statement P_m is true. However, given step 2
above, that leads to a contradiction.

Let's take a look at a proof by induction to clarify the situation somewhat.
I begin with the following situation:

> I have a lot of blocks that are either red and blue in color and, using only
> these colors, I wish to build all possible towers of height 4. How many
> such towers are there?

P R O B L E M   1 . 4

Write this problem on a piece of paper. Close this book and attempt your own systematic
solution.

If I list the towers—in essence, a proof by exhaustion—I have symbolically
(R indicates a red block and B indicates a blue block) the following:

R R R R R R R R B B B B B B B B
R R R R B B B B R R R R B B B B
R R B B R R B B R R B B R R B B
R B R B R B R B R B R B R B R B

which indicates that there are 16 possibilities.

If I attempted the problem for towers of height 5, I would find that there were 32 possibilities. This suggests that the number of towers N high is 2^N. This is a reasonable conjecture, but I need to *prove* it. An inductive proof might run roughly as follows:

Step 1: For towers 1 block high, I have just the red block or the blue block. That is two possibilities in all, and $2^1 = 2$. So my formula works for towers 1 high.

Step 2: I need to show if 2^n is the number of towers that are n high, then 2^{n+1} is the number of towers that are $n + 1$ high. So I imagine I have a room full of all the towers —2^n towers of them—that are n high. To make towers $n + 1$ high, I can add either a red or a blue to the top of each of these towers. Say I add a red to the top of all of these towers. I now have 2^n towers $n + 1$ high with a red on the top. Likewise, if I add a blue, I then have 2^n towers $n + 1$ high with a blue on the top. Together these are all my possible towers that are $n + 1$ blocks high:

$$
\begin{array}{ccc}
\text{red} & & \text{blue} \\
\text{top} & & \text{top} \\
2^n & + & 2^n = 2 \cdot 2^n \\
& & = 2^{n+1}
\end{array}
$$

as was to be shown.

P R O B L E M   1 . 5

Give a proof by induction that if you are allowed to use only blocks of red, blue, and green, the number of possible towers N blocks high is 3^N.

Proofs by Contradiction

A proof by contradiction establishes the truth of a statement by assuming the statement is false and, on the basis of this assumption, deducing a contradiction. Consider the following vignette:

Susie comes up to your desk. "Mr. Bass," she says, "I have a conjecture. We've been talking about primes. Y'know those numbers that are only divisible by themselves and one. Like 19! I've been experimenting. I don't think any of the numbers between 1 and 11 are differences of two primes." Mr. Bass thinks for a moment and says, "What about 3 minus 2?" Susie frowns, "I thought you said we didn't have to do 1, but anyway I said 'between 1 and 11.' So I think this [and she points at the 1] is the only one." Mr. Bass smiles and asks, "Is this another conjecture?" Susie smiles and replies, "Not yet. I need to experiment more." Mr. Bass says, "Okay. How about 5 minus 3." Susie frowns and says, "I forgot about 2 because it is so weird. An even prime! But I'm pretty sure about the rest [she sounds unsure]. Oh no! I just realized that 23 minus 13 is 10! I guess it isn't a good conjecture." Mr. Bass smiles. "Perhaps we should get the rest of the class to help. Okay, how about something like . . . [and here he writes and says]:

Susie's Question

What numbers between 1 and 11 are not the difference of two primes? Prove your answers.

Then he smiles and says, "Do you want to include that business about 1?" Susie giggles, "Yes!" so Mr. Bass adds

Susie's Conjecture

The only time 1 is the difference of two primes is when the primes are 2 and 3 (2 minus 1 doesn't count). Prove your answer.

P R O B L E M   1 . 6

Write Susie's question and Susie's conjecture on a piece of paper. Close this book and attempt your own systematic solutions.

Most children (and many adults) who attempt to answer Susie's question notice that

$$5 - 3 = 2 \qquad 7 - 3 = 4 \qquad 17 - 11 = 6 \qquad 13 - 5 = 8 \qquad 17 - 7 = 10$$
$$5 - 2 = 3 \qquad 7 - 2 = 5 \qquad\qquad\qquad 11 - 2 = 9$$

but then are unable to find two primes whose difference is 7. This does seem to indicate that 7 is indeed the only number between 1 and 11 that is not the difference of two primes. However, there are a lot of primes, and clearly we can't try them all. To remedy this, let me give a proof by contradiction:

I begin by assuming the contrary. I assume that there are indeed two primes x and y whose difference is 7. That is,

$$x - y = 7$$

Note that this implies that

$$x = y + 7$$

Now 7 is odd[7] and I have two cases:

Case 1: If y is odd, then x must be even and a prime. That is possible only if x is 2. However, it is clear that x is greater than 7. So y cannot be odd.

Case 2: So y must be even. That is, y must be 2. Thus x must be 9. However, although 9 is odd, 9 is not a prime.

---

[7] Note that at this point, I am giving postulational proofs.

Thus I have a contradiction, and hence, 7 is not the difference of two primes.

Susie's conjecture can be settled in a similar fashion:

Assume Susie's conjecture is untrue. Then there is a pair of primes x and y other than 2 and 3 such that

$$x - y = 1$$

Note that this implies that

$$x = y + 1$$

I have two cases:

Case 1: If y is even—that is, if y is 2—then x is 3. I have, however, assumed that this is not the case.

Case 2: So y must be odd. However, since an odd number plus an odd number is even, x must be even. That is, x must be 2. This implies that y must be 1. This, however, was disallowed in the statement of Susie's conjecture.

Thus I have a contradiction, and hence, Susie's conjecture must be true.

Investigations

1. I have pennies, nickels, and dimes in my pocket. I pull three coins from my pocket and double the value of one coin. (a) How many different amounts could I have? (b) Give a convincing proof by exhaustion that you have them all.
2. You have two whole numbers x and y such that $2 < x$ and $2 < y$. Assume that for any three whole numbers a, b (b non-zero), z,

   If $a < z$, then $a \cdot b < b \cdot z$

   Give a convincing postulational proof that $4 < x \cdot y$.
3. While building trains with equilateral triangles with unit sides, as follows,

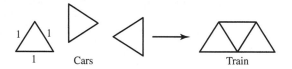

Cars   Train

   you notice that the perimeter P of the train appears to be given by

   $$P = T + 2$$

   where T is the number of triangles.
   Prove, using induction, that this is indeed the case.
4. Prove that $n^2 \geq 2n$ for 2, 3, 4, 5 . . . . [*Hint:* Use a proof by induction.]
5. Prove that there is no largest integer. [*Hint:* Use a proof by contradiction.]

Counting and Recording of Numbers

The art of counting and recording numbers is one of the oldest mathematical skills for which we have evidence. In fact, there is some evidence that it preceded written language.[1] In this chapter, I will briefly review for you some historical and developmental aspects of this art, and then, before taking up positional systems and the representation of large numbers, I will show you how some of the ideas behind this art can be represented with the notations of set and function.

✂ Numbers and Counting from a Historical Perspective

The use of marks or notches to denote numbers was probably among the first numeric representational systems (see Figure 2.1).

FIGURE 2.1.   *A Tally Stick*

The Roman numerals I, II, and III may be a quite literal means of recording such notching, and it seems possible that certain of the other symbols—for example, X—were chosen to facilitate reading of the tally marks when they became numerous. That is, each X, or cross-notch, stands for a group of ten notches.

Let's take a look at how some of these early recording systems worked.[2] One of the earliest was the Egyptian recording system (ca. 3400 BC) shown in Figure 2.2.

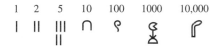

FIGURE 2.2   *Early Egyptian Numerals*

---

[1] Consider, for example, the use of first, second, and third person.
[2] My presentation here is taken largely from Oystein Ore, *Number Theory and Its History* (New York: McGraw-Hill, 1948), pp. 10–30.

In this system, 1867, for example, would be written as

$$
\text{DA}\ \begin{matrix}
\text{\textsection\textsection\textsection} & \cap\cap & || \\
\text{\textsection\textsection\textsection} & \cap\cap & ||| \\
\text{\textsection\textsection} & \cap\cap & ||
\end{matrix}
$$

Then we have the Roman system, which may have been in use as early as 800 BC (see Figure 2.3).

1	2	5	10	50	100	500	1000
I	II	V	X	L	C	D	M

FIGURE 2.3   *Roman Numerals*

In this system, 1867 would be written as

MDCCCLXVII

The Roman symbols L and D, corresponding to 50 and 500, respectively, simplify the writing of numbers. The subtraction principle in Roman numerals (for instance, IX = 9 and IV = 4) may have a similar function.

Attic Greek numerals, which may have been in use as early as 700 BC, are employed in a manner somewhat similar to Roman numerals (see Figure 2.4).

1	5	10	100	1000	10,000
I	Γ	Δ	H	Χ	M

FIGURE 2.4   *Attic Greek Numerals*

In this system, 1867 might be written as

Χ ₣ H H H Δ Δ Δ Δ Δ Δ Γ I I

Note that the composite numeral ₣ now represents $5 \cdot 100$.

The Egyptian, Roman, and Attic Greek recording systems are *simple grouping systems* that use repetition of symbols to denote multiplication—that is, XXX corresponds to 30. The traditional *Chinese–Japanese numeral system* (see Figure 2.5) is a true multiplicative grouping system. Such multiplicative systems were in use as early as 1400 BC.

1	2	3	4	5	6	7	8	9	10	100	1000	10,000
一	二	三	四	五	六	七	八	九	十	百	千	百

FIGURE 2.5   *Chinese–Japanese Numerals*

In this system, writing is vertical instead of horizontal. Thus 1867 would be written as

一
千
八
百
六
十
七

There is a third method of number recording called a *ciphered numeral system*. In the case of a decadic system, or ten system, the numbers from 1 to 9 are written with special symbols and, similarly, so are the tens up to 90 and the hundreds up to 900. In such a system, all numbers can be represented as a combination of symbols in a very compact form. The Greek alphabetical numerals (ca. 400 BC) are of this type (see Figure 2.6).[3]

1–9	α	β	γ	δ	ε	ς	ζ	η	θ
10–90	ι	κ	λ	μ	ν	ξ	ο	π	ϙ
100–900	ρ	σ	τ	υ	φ	χ	ψ	ω	ϡ

FIGURE 2.6   *Greek Alphabetic Numerals*

The higher units were obtained by adding special marks after the symbol for the lower unit. For example,

$$,\alpha = 1000$$

so 1867 might be written as

$$,\alpha\omega\xi\zeta$$

P R O B L E M   2 . 1

Write 759 (a) using Greek alphabetic numerals; (b) Roman numerals. What are the advantages and disadvantages of each system?

The numerals we now use are commonly known as the Hindu-Arabic numerals because historical evidence points to India as their origin.[4] The Arabs, however, were instrumental in their transmission to Europe. One form of these Hindu numerals—the Gobar (or dust) numerals—was introduced by the Arabs

---

[3] Oystein Ore, *Number Theory and Its History* (New York: McGraw-Hill, 1948), p. 13.
[4] The use of a positional system with zero appears to have occurred in India as early as AD 600.

into Spain as early as AD 1000. The way these numerals were written is quite similar to how we write our numerals today (see Figure 2.7).[5]

FIGURE 2.7   *Gobar Arabic Numerals*

⚔ Numbers and Counting from a Developmental Perspective

There is substantial evidence that counting is a natural human endeavor and that children in their early months are able to discriminate, for example, one object from two objects. Around the age of two or three, the average child begins to be able to compare larger groups of objects. However, it is around the age of four to five that something remarkable happens. Children consistently begin to demonstrate a sense of ordinality—that is, they count in a sequential fashion—and children begin to exhibit an understanding of cardinality. That is, they begin to understand that the number of objects they have counted, assuming the sequence of objects is taken in a fixed order and they begin with 1, can be labeled by the last ordinal number in a counting sequence.[6]

Even though these emerging abilities are something that we, as accomplished counters, often take for granted, they are indicative of an intuitive skillfulness with some rather deep mathematics. Let's take a look.[7]

Five-year-old Peter is playing with some cars as Ms. Jannat approaches. She has a tin canister in her hand, and as she sits beside him on the floor, she asks, "Do you know what I have in the can?" Peter shakes his head and Ms. Jannat says "Candies." She takes the lid from the canister and tilts the container toward Peter, saying, "How many do you think there are?" Peter looks into the can and, carefully touching each of the wrapped candies (not an easy task), he counts, "One, two, three, four, five, six." Ms. Jannat smiles and pours the candies out on the floor near the cars. One candy falls behind a car. She says "Are you sure?" Peter moves the candy that has fallen behind a car so it is together with the rest, and he again counts. He then lines the candies in a column—the two blue candies are at the top—and, as he counts, he tags each candy with a number, "One, two, three, four, five, six, seven." "How many?" Ms. Jannat asks. Peter again begins to count, "One, two, three." He hesitates and then he says, "Seven."

---

[5] Oystein Ore, *Number Theory and Its History*, p. 20.
[6] For a detailed discussion of these *principles*—static order, one-to-one, and cardinality—see Catherine Sophian, *The Origins of Mathematical Knowledge in Children* (New York: Lawrence Erlbaum, 2007).
[7] This vignette is adapted from Sherrin B. Hersch, Antonia Cameron, Maarten Dolk, and Catherine Twomey Fosnot, *Fostering Children's Mathematical Development, Grades PreK–3* (Portsmouth, NH: Heinemann, 2004).

❈ The Art of Counting

From a mathematical point of view, we might say that Peter understands that if he wishes to count any group or set of objects, he can apply one and only one number name to each object. Obvious, isn't it. Let's look still deeper.

Sets

Before Peter even begins to count, he must have some idea of what constitutes a *counting* object and what constitutes a group or set of objects to be counted. In this instance each object is represented by a candy, and the set of objects is represented by those particular candies that were in the tin canister. That is,

        is an object or an element

and

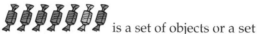 is a set of objects or a set

Because Peter seems to know all this, we might not be surprised if he could also count the two sets

if these sets were put together on a plate or the tabletop.

    Now let me complicate things slightly. Say I give Andre, a second grader, two lists or sets of names:

Boys in the Classroom	Children Who Are Seven Years Old in the Classroom
Derrick	Samantha
Steve	Steve
John	Jelisa
	Tiffany
	Lai Ling

and ask him to count how many children there are in total—that is, to count the union (denoted by ∪) of the two sets or lists. Presumably, he would, in effect, count Derrick, Steve (noting that Steve is in both lists), John, Samantha, Jelisa, Tiffany, and Lai Ling. On the other hand, suppose I asked him to count all the boys who are seven years old—that is, to count the intersection (denoted by ∩) of the two lists. Presumably, he would count only Steve.

    I might represent the answers to these two questions mathematically by writing

    {Derrick, Steve, John} ∪ {Samantha, Steve, Jelisa, Tiffany, Lai Ling}

      = {Derrick, Steve, John, Samantha, Jelisa, Tiffany, Lai Ling} and

{Derrick, Steve, John} ∩ {Samantha, Steve, Jelisa, Tiffany, Lai Ling} = {Steve}

I can also (and this representation can be used in the primary grades) use a Venn diagram and compactly represent both the union and the intersection:

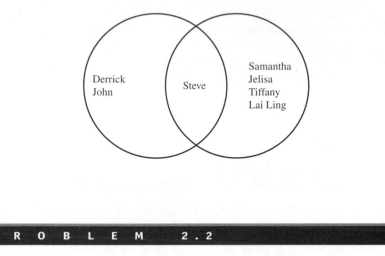

P R O B L E M   2 . 2

Out of 70 people, 34 jog, 25 bowl, 27 ski, 7 jog and bowl, 11 jog and ski, 6 ski and bowl, and 5 do all three activities.

    a. Construct and label an appropriate Venn diagram.

    b. How many do none of the activities?

    c. How many bowl but do not ski?

The notations for operations on sets can be extended somewhat. I might ask Andre to count the number of children who are boys but are not seven years old. I write this as

{Derrick, Steve, John} − {Samantha, Steve, Jelisa, Tiffany, Lai Ling}

It is evident from the Venn diagram that the answer would be just Derrick and John.

P R O B L E M   2 . 3

Let the set $T = \{1, 2, 3, 4\}$ and the set $S = \{-1, 3, 4\}$. Compute:

    a. $T \cap S$

    b. $T \cup S$

    c. $T - S$

Functions

The next challenge Peter faces is to correctly tag each of the candies with an appropriate number.[8] That is,

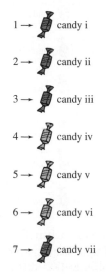

1 → candy i

2 → candy ii

3 → candy iii

4 → candy iv

5 → candy v

6 → candy vi

7 → candy vii

In this case, we say that there is a function f mapping the set of counting numbers $S = \{1, 2, 3, 4, 5, 6, 7\}$ to the set of candies $C = \{$candy i, candy ii, candy iii, candy iv, candy v, candy vi, candy vii$\}$ so that for an element x of S, $f(x) =$ candy x.

Initially, however, as we recall, Peter somehow undercounted. That is, he failed to tag one of the candies. For instance, he might have tagged the candies as follows:

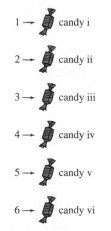

1 → candy i

2 → candy ii

3 → candy iii

4 → candy iv

5 → candy v

6 → candy vi

---

[8] It seems possible that all this might build on children's earlier attempts to compare different groups of objects. Here, rather than matching to another group of objects, a child matches to what appears to be a finite subset of the counting numbers.

or he might have tagged them as follows:

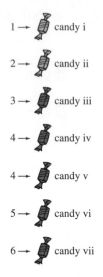

$1 \rightarrow$ candy i

$2 \rightarrow$ candy ii

$3 \rightarrow$ candy iii

$4 \rightarrow$ candy iv

$4 \rightarrow$ candy v

$5 \rightarrow$ candy vi

$6 \rightarrow$ candy vii

Neither of these tagging schemes is a function from S, the domain, to C, the codomain, because the first scheme omits a counting number, and the second assigns the same counting number to two different candies.

Notice that rather than undercounting, he might have tagged one candy twice. For example,

$1 \,\&\, 4 \rightarrow$ candy i

It this case, he would have overcounted. Although this tagging scheme is a function, it is not what is termed a one-to-one function. That is, there is not one and only one counting number assigned to each candy. The range of f (that is, the set of actual values of f) is R = {candy i, candy ii, candy iii, candy v, candy vi, candy vii}, and that range R is a proper subset of C = {candy i, candy ii, candy iii, candy iv, candy v, candy vi, candy vii}.

PROBLEM 2.4

Let S = {1, 2, 3, 4, 5} and let C = {1, 2, 4, 6, 8, 11} and define the relationship F mapping the elements of S to the elements of C by

$$F(x) = 2x$$

a. Is F a function with domain S and codomain C? Why or why not?

b. Let $P = S - \{5\}$. Is F a function with domain P and codomain C? Why or why not?

c. Let $Q = C - \{11\}$. Then F is a function with domain P and codomain Q. Is F a one-to-one function? Why or why not?

The function notation provides a nice way of specifying arithmetic rules. For example, say we wish to write a function, F, that has domain and range equal to the counting numbers and that gives the sum of any sequence of counting numbers beginning with 1. I conjecture that a function that will do this is

Number of Addends

1   $F(1) = 1$
2   $F(2) = 1 + 2 = 3$
3   $F(3) = 1 + 2 + 3 = 6$

$\vdots$

n $F(n) = 1 + 2 + \cdots + n = \dfrac{n(n + 1)}{2}$

How do you know I'm right? A few calculations should convince you that this function seems to work. However, that is not enough. You need to prove or disprove my conjecture. I'm going to do an inductive proof (you may wish to review proof by induction in Chapter 1). Now (step 1)

$$F(1) = \frac{1(1 + 1)}{2} = 1$$

So my function works for 1. Thus I'll assume (step 2) that

Induction proof

$$F(n) = \frac{n(n + 1)}{2}$$

for $1 \le n < N$ for some arbitrary N and then prove that

$$F(N + 1) = \frac{(N + 1)(N + 2)}{2}$$

Well,

$$F(N + 1) = 1 + 2 + \cdots + N + (N + 1)$$
$$= F(N) + (N + 1)$$

However, I know that

$$F(N) = \frac{(N)(N + 1)}{2}$$

so

$$F(N + 1) = \frac{N(N + 1)}{2} + (N + 1) = \frac{N(N + 1)}{2} + \frac{2(N + 1)}{2}$$

Using the distributive rule gives me

$$F(N + 1) = \frac{(N + 1)(N + 2)}{2}$$

as was to be shown.

P R O B L E M   2 . 5

What is the sum of the whole numbers from 1 to 102 (that is, $1 + 2 + \cdots + 102$)?

Combinatorics

Notions of sets and functions give rise, as they naturally should, to further mathematical questions. For example, I might wonder in how many ways could Peter count those seven candies. For example, he might count beginning at candy i and count continuing to candy vii:

$$i, ii, iii, iv, v, vi, vii \qquad\qquad (A)$$

or he might begin at candy ii, continue to candy vii, and count candy i last:

$$ii, iii, iv, v, vi, vii, i \qquad\qquad (B)$$

Sequence B is called a *permutation* of sequence A. Thus I might rephrase my initial question and wonder how many permutations there are of the seven symbols representing these seven candies.[9]

Let me, so as to conserve space, try this for three symbols i, ii, iii. I can begin with any of these three symbols, and after using a symbol, I cannot use it again. Thus the possible permutations are

Count 1	Count 2	Count 3
i	ii	iii
i	iii	ii
ii	iii	i
ii	i	iii
iii	i	ii
iii	ii	i

That is, I can choose among three possibilities for count 1, and once I have chosen which object I tag with that first count, I must choose between the two other possibilities for count 2. When the first and second counts are fixed, there is only one possibility for count 3. Therefore, the number of possible permutations with three objects is

$$3 \cdot 2 \cdot 1 = 6$$

and the possible number of permutations with seven objects is

$$7 \cdot 6 \cdot 5 \cdot 4 \cdot 3 \cdot 2 \cdot 1 = 5040$$

That is, Peter could count the seven candies in 5040 ways.

P R O B L E M   2 . 6

I have four shirts, two pairs of pants, and two pairs of shoes. How many outfits could I create? (An outfit consists of a pair of shoes, a pair of pants, and one shirt.)

---

[9] Such a mathematical move has been termed mathematizing. The introduction of symbols is to represent the candies for mathematical purposes. Such symbols no longer retain the color, the wrapping, or the taste of what they represent.

⚔ Positional Number Systems

The *number zero* is crucial to the number system we use today. The availability of zero is something we take for granted today, but its introduction was a major mathematical accomplishment. Zero enables us to use an efficient positional notation to write numbers. For example, rather than representing one thousand, nine hundred, sixty-five as MCMLXV, we write 1965.

How does it work? Each digit in a numeral has a value that is, in effect, given by the value of the digit times the value of its place in the numeral. Thus, for example, the leftmost digit in 1965 is a 1, and it is in the fourth place, so its value is $1 \cdot 10^3$, or one thousand. In like manner, the 9 has the value of $9 \cdot 10^2$ (that is, nine hundred), the 6 has the value $6 \cdot 10^1$ (that is, sixty), and the 5 has the value $5 \cdot 10^0$ (that is, five). All this implies that zero is not merely a *placeholder* when it is used as a digit in a number (for example, 405) to indicate that there are zero of that positional value (for example, in *expanded notation*, $405 = 4 \cdot 10^2 + \underline{0} \cdot 10^1 + 5 \cdot 10^0$). We term such a number system a base-10 system because it consists of the ten digits 0, 1, 2, 3, 4, 5, 6, 7, 8, and 9 *and* positional values that are powers of 10 (that is, 10^0, 10^1, 10^2 10^3, ...).

The base-10 number system is the positional number system we normally use to do arithmetic, but there are several other positional number systems that have practical application. Computers use a base-2 (or binary) number system to a large extent, and programmers use base-8 and base-16 number systems from time to time. There are also vestiges of base-5 (penny, nickels, and quarters) and base-60 (clock arithmetic) number systems in practical use. How do they work? The simple answer is that they work exactly the same as our base-10 system.

Let me give a somewhat deeper answer for a base-6 system. Our digits will be 0, 1, 2, 3, 4, 5 (six in all) and the value of the places from right to left will be 6^0, 6^1, 6^2, 6^3, ... Thus the number 123_6 (here the subscript 6 indicates that this is a number written in base-6) has, using *expanded notation*, the value in base-10 of $1 \cdot 6^2 + 2 \cdot 6^1 + 3 \cdot 6^0$, or $1 \cdot 36 + 2 \cdot 6 + 3$, or, in base 10, 51. We can check all this for smaller numbers, say 12_6 (which a similar calculation shows to be 8) by counting:

Base-6	Base-10
0	0
1	1
2	2
3	3
4	4
5	5
10	6
11	7
12	8

Note the rollover (much like the rollover when we add 1 to 9 in base 10) to 10_6 when we add 1 to 5 in base-6.

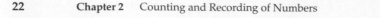

P R O B L E M   2 . 7

In base-6, how would you write the numerical sum of 3 and 4?

___

Base-2, for instance, is especially simple because we have only the digits 0 and 1 and each place has a value given by the appropriate power of 2. For example, 10101_2 would have, in base 10, the value $1 \cdot 2^4 + 0 \cdot 2^3 + 1 \cdot 2^2 + 0 \cdot 2^1 + 1$, or $16 + 4$, or, in base-10, the value 20. To illustrate, let's check to see that 111_2 counts 7 in base 10

Base-2	Base-10
0	0
1	1
10	2
11	3
100	4
101	5
110	6
111	7

As indicated, we can convert, for example, from base-6 to base-10. For instance, in *expanded notation* we have

$$124_6 = 1 \cdot 6^2 + 2 \cdot 6^1 + 4 \cdot 6^0$$
$$= 52_{10}$$

How does one convert from, say, base-6 to base-8? To understand how to do this, we need to return to the first grade classroom. Our problem is much like that of a first grader who wants to represent, in base-10, the number of sticks in a pile. Our imaginary first grader—let's call her Taya—might proceed as follows:
    There are 112 sticks in the pile.

- Taya counts the sticks carefully and bundles them in groups of ten. At this point she has eleven bundles of 10 and 2 loose sticks, so she writes 2 in the ones place.
- She now bundles the bundles of 10 in bundles of 10. She now has one bundle of 100 and one leftover bundle of 10, so she places 1 in the tens place.
- And since she cannot make any bundles of 1000, she places 1 in the hundreds place.

Let me show you how to convert 33_6 to base-2 using Taya's method. In base-10 expanded notation,[10]

$$33_6 = 3 \cdot 6^1 + 3$$

___

[10] Note that if you expanded 33_6 in base-6, you would have $33_6 = 3 \cdot (10_6)^1 + 3 \cdot (10_6)^0$.

so I have 21 sticks in my pile. Now

$$21 = 10 \cdot 2 + \underline{1}$$

Thus I have ten bundles of 2 and 1 loose stick. Bundling these ten bundles of 2 into bundles of 2, I have five bundles—five bundles of $2 \cdot 2$:

$$10 = 5 \cdot 2 + \underline{0}$$

and no bundles of $2 \cdot 2$ left over. Bundling these five bundles of $2 \cdot 2$ into bundles of 2, I have two bundles—two bundles of $2 \cdot 2 \cdot 2$:

$$5 = 2 \cdot 2 + \underline{1}$$

and one bundle of $2 \cdot 2$ left over, and bundling those two bundles of $2 \cdot 2 \cdot 2$ into bundles of $2 \cdot 2 \cdot 2 \cdot 2$, I have one bundle of $2 \cdot 2 \cdot 2 \cdot 2$ and no bundles of $2 \cdot 2 \cdot 2$ left over:

$$2 = 1 \cdot 2 + \underline{0}$$

Hence, as I have only one bundle of $2 \cdot 2 \cdot 2 \cdot 2$ remaining:

$$33_6 = 10101_2$$

P R O B L E M   2 . 8

Convert 33_6 to base-8.

❄ Large Numbers

Out of counting grow natural questions about big numbers. How big is a billion? What is the largest number you can write? What is the largest number you can know? Do numbers go on forever? Through the use of zero and commas, children learn how to write a billion:

$$1,000,000,000$$

and at a later point, they learn that this can be written more compactly in expanded notation, as 10^9.

However, in a mathematical sense, even something like $10^{1,000,000,000}$ is rather small. Some notation that we owe to Leo Moser enables us to go further. I define

$$\boxed{\triangle\; a} = a^a \quad \text{For example,} \quad \triangle\; 2 = 2^2 = 4.$$

and

$$\boxed{b} = b \text{ with } b \;\triangle\text{'s around it.}$$

For example, $\boxed{2}$ = (triangle with 2 inside) = (triangle with 4 inside) $= 4^4 = 256.$

Now let (pentagon with c inside) $= c$ with c $\Box$'s around it.

Moser defined a mega as (hexagon with 2 inside), and, not content to let large alone, he continued the above pattern with hexagons, heptagons, and so on. That is, he defined recursively[11] an n-gon containing the number d as d with $(n-1)$-gons around it. A moser is defined as 2 inside a megagon. How big is a mega? Well,

(pentagon with 2 inside) = $\boxed{\boxed{2}}$ = $\boxed{256}$

= 256 with 256 (triangle)'s around it

Let me try to convince you that this is large beyond imagining. I'll start small.

$\boxed{10}$ = 10 with 10 (triangle)'s around it

= 10,000,000,000 with 9 (triangle)'s around it

= $10,000,000,000^{10,000,000,000}$ with 8 (triangle)'s around it

= $10^{100,000,000,000}$ with 8 (triangle)'s around it

Have I convinced you? The number of atoms in our universe is, by the way, estimated to be somewhat less than 10^{81}.

Investigations

1. Outline the history of Roman numerals from their earliest use to the present.
2. (a) Use a Venn diagram to demonstrate that for any two sets A and B,

$$A \cup B = (A - B) \cup (A \cap B) \cup (B - A)$$

---

[11] That is, the value of each regular enclosing polygon of n sides in terms of the appropriate number of nested polygons of $n - 1$ sides.

(b) Two sets C and D are said to be equal if every element of C is an element of D and if every element of D is an element of C. Use this definition of equality to *prove* (it would be good to think about the Venn diagram) that

$$A \cup B = (A - B) \cup (A \cap B) \cup (B - A)$$

3. If I have 112 sticks, then it is clear, as Taya has shown above, that this can be written as 112_{10}. However, I could have counted by ones or skip-counted by twos, so how do I know this representation is unique? Might I, in fact, be able to record, within the usual notation of base 10, this pile of sticks in two different ways? Prove that this cannot be the case—that is, prove that the representation of any number in base 10 is unique. [*Hint:* A reasonable way to go about this is a proof by contradiction. That is, assume $112 = abc$, where a, b, c are the usual base-10 digits, and show you get a contradiction if a is not 1, b is not 1, or c is not 2.]

4. (a) Write a line of 8s and add plus signs so that the resulting sum is 1000. What are all the different solutions?[12] [*Hint:* There are more than ten.]
   (b) Give a convincing proof by exhaustion that you have them all.

5. The distance from the earth to the sun is approximately 150×10^6 kilometers. Say you walk there at a speed of 5 kilometers per hour (roughly 3 miles per hour). How many minutes would your journey take? How many years?

---

[12] Devised by Hyman Bass.

Sums

The focus of this chapter is on the art of making sums—that is, finding solutions to problems of the form

$$5 + 4 = x$$

You and I will first examine this art historically and developmentally, and then we will take a closer look at the general-purpose standard addition algorithm

$$
\begin{array}{r}
{\scriptstyle 1} \\
153 \\
+273 \\
\hline
426
\end{array}
$$

This will be followed by a glimpse into methods for summing certain series of integers—for example, the odd numbers:

$$1 + 3 + 5 + 7 + \cdots$$

and a glimpse into methods for systematically determining integer solutions to certain linear sums—for instance, third grade word problems of the following form:

> Pencils cost 15 cents and erasers cost 10 cents. If you are to spend exactly $2.00 (forget about tax), what are the different combinations of pencils and erasers that you can buy?

✼ Addition from a Historical Perspective

How addition was conceptualized in ancient times remains elusive, because until more recent times, few written records were kept describing the process. Much of what we know about early practices of addition comes from speculating on the use of early calculating devices and examining historical financial accounts. The ration tablet shown in Figure 3.1, a representation of a clay tablet from the Yale Babylonian Collection,[1] is a typical example. The double line dividing the top row from the rest of the tablet indicates that there are two

---

[1] Dated around 3000 BC.

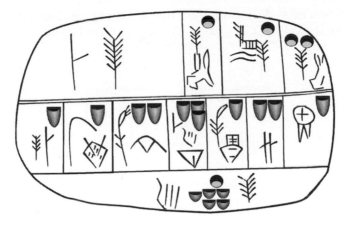

FIGURE 3.1   *A Babylonian Ration Tablet*

different accounts. In the bottom account, there are seven disbursements of dif-
fering amounts, of 1, 2, or 3 wedges of grain for a total in that account of 11
wedges. The lowest row gives the sum of these accounts: a circle and 5 wedges.[2]

Approximately 2500 years later, Herodotus provides, in his writings, a
description of the differences between Greek and Egyptian reckoning utilizing the counting board or loose-counter abacus.[3] This device was a flat surface
marked with a series of parallel lines that were labeled, for instance, in increas-
ing order by 1, 10, 100, and 1000. The counters were small pebbles or disks about
the size of a penny. Figure 3.2 is a schematic representation of what the device
looked like in Roman times. Although we know little about its actual operation,
the manner in which a modern abacus is used provides some reasonable clues.

```
 _____
|  ___   ___   ___   ___   ___   ___   ___  |
| | o | | o | | o | | o | | o | | o | | o | |
|  ---   ---   ---   ---   ---   ---   ---  |
 ---------------------------------------

 _____
| MM    CM    XM    M     C     X     I     |
| --    --    --    -     -     -     -     |
|  |     |     |     |     |     |     |    |
|  |     |     |     |     |     |     |    |
|  o     o     o     o     o     o     o    |
|  o     o     o     o     o     o     o    |
|  o     o     o     o     o     o     o    |
| |o|   |o|   |o|   |o|   |o|   |o|   |o|   |
 ---------------------------------------
```

FIGURE 3.2   *The Roman Counting Board*

Let's assume that the board shown in Figure 3.2 represents zero. Each pebble in the lower half of the counting board will have, when moved upward, the
value of 1 times the labeled unit, and each pebble in the upper half of the board

---

[2] There is evidence that a circle in this context is equivalent to 6 wedges.
[3] See Vera Sanford, "Counters: Computing If You Can Count to Five." In *From Five Fingers to Infinity: A Journey through the History of Mathematics*, ed. Frank J. Swetz (Chicago: Open Court, 1994).

will have, when moved upward, the value of 5 times the labeled unit. Thus, I can represent the value CLIII (that is, 153) as shown in Figure 3.3.

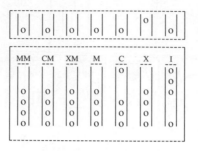

FIGURE 3.3   *CLIII*

If I wish to add CCLXXIII (that is, 273), I proceed as follows:

- I add 3 by pushing up the 5 pebble in the "I" column and returning two of the 1 pebbles to their zero position. At this point I have the intermediate result of 156.
- I add 70 by returning the 50 pebble—in the "X" column—to its zero position and then adding 20 more. Returning the 50 pebble to its zero position results in a carry to the "C" column. Adding 20 more pushes up two of the 10 pebbles. The carry to the "C" column results in one of the 100 pebbles being pushed up, with the intermediate result of 226.
- Finally I add 200 by pushing up two of the 100 pebbles in the "C" column and have a final result of 426 (that is, CDXXVI); see Figure 3.4.

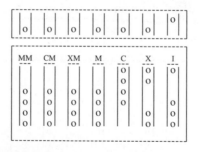

FIGURE 3.4   *CDXXVI*

P R O B L E M   3 . 1

Make a quick sketch of a counting board by labeling some parallel lines 1, 10, 100, 1000. Using some slideable object for your counters, try the following calculations: (a) 22 + 47; (b) 36 + 15; (c) 196 + 54; (d) something daring.

Note that Roman numerals seem particularly well suited to the counting board because, for instance, 7 is just 5 + 2 (that is, VII) and 9 is 10 − 1 (that is IX).

Although the counting board and the later abacus remained a principal computational device well into the sixteenth century, the precursors of the standard addition algorithm began appearing in various arithmetics by the fifteenth century. One of these—*The Craft of Nombrynge* (an interpretation of Alexander de Villa Dei's *Canto of Algorismo*)—reads as follows:[4]

> Here begins the craft of addition. In this craft you must know four things. First you must know what is addition. Next you must know how many rows of figures you must have. Next you must know how many different cases happen in this craft. And next what is the result of this craft. As for the first you must know that addition is a summing together of two numbers into one number. As for the second you must know that you will have two rows of figures, one under the other as here you may see:
>
> 123
> 234
>
> As for the third you must know that there are four different cases. As for the fourth you must know that the result of this craft is to tell what is the whole number that comes of summing these different numbers.

The four cases of which Alexander de Villa writes are

1. No partial sum (that is, $1 + 2, 2 + 3$, or $3 + 4$ in the passage above) is greater than 9.
2. At least one partial sum is greater than 9.
3. At least one partial sum is 10 or a multiple of 10.
4. There is a zero in the upper row.

P R O B L E M   3 . 2

Illustrate each of the four cases with an additive example.

In present times these cases have been consolidated—the designation of carries is a product of more modern times—into that polished and efficient piece of mathematical machinery we term the standard addition algorithm. That is,

$$\begin{array}{r} {\scriptstyle 1} \\ 153 \\ +273 \\ \hline 426 \end{array}$$

⚔ Addition from a Developmental Perspective

Moving from counting to addition is somewhat of a natural progression. Children often go from counting one set of blocks to counting two sets of blocks by physically forming the union of the sets and, beginning at a first

---

[4] Rewritten in American English of the late twentieth century in Robert Steele (ed.), *The Earliest Arithmetics in English* (Oxford: Oxford University Press, 1922).

block in the combined set, counting "One, two, three, four, five, six, seven, eight, nine."

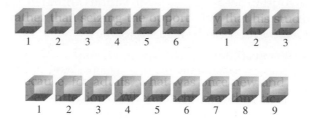

As children become more at ease with notions of cardinality (that is, as they realize that the last number counted within a set is the number of objects in that set), they begin *counting on*. To do this a child must first hold the cardinality of the first set of objects in her mind, and then, beginning with some first element in the second set, count on from the cardinality of the first set "<u>Six</u>, seven, eight, nine."

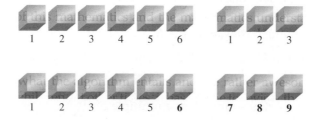

In U.S. schools, children are consolidating these experiences and committing them to remembrance at the end of first grade and into second grade. Typically, addition facts within 5—for example, $1 + 4 = 5$ and $2 + 2 = 4$—are learned first, followed by facts within 10 and then facts within 20. There is some speculation that U.S. children may, perhaps because of the irregular words we use for counting, be at a disadvantage compared to their Asian peers.[5] In such parts of the world (typically in first grade), children are taught to *make ten* when adding:

$$6 + 5 \text{ becomes } 1 + (5 + 5)$$

Intriguingly, this strategy might also be employed when using the abacus. Some Japanese adults, in fact, report adding $6 + 3$ by thinking or visualizing

$$(5 + 1) + 3$$

P R O B L E M   3 . 3

If order is irrelevant, how many different addition facts would a child need to memorize to (a) make 5; (b) make 6; (c) make 10?

---

[5] K. C. Fuson, "Developing mathematical power in whole number operations." In *A Research Companion to NCTM's Standards*, ed J. Kilpatrick, W. G. Martin, and D. Schifter (Reston, VA: NCTM, 2003), p. 74.

Addition facts, together with notions such as commutativity

$$2 + 5 = 5 + 2$$

and associativity

$$(2 + 5) + 3 = 2 + (5 + 3)$$

are foundational in the art of making sums.

In the United States, usually by the end of second grade and into third grade, children begin practicing multi-row and multi-column addition. As an illustration, consider the following vignette.[6]

Mr. Daley's second graders have been working on addition. Mr. Daley has posed the following addition problem to his class:

> We have 153 students at our school. There are 273 students at the school down the street. How many students are there in both schools?

and has asked them to model and record their strategies.

His students give a variety of responses that illustrate a range of understandings. For example (see Figure 3.5), Randy models the problem with base-10 blocks, using hundreds flats, tens longs, and ones cubes. He models the numbers and combines blocks, but he is not certain how to record the results. He draws a picture of the base-10 blocks and labels the parts "3 flats," "12 longs," "6 cubes."

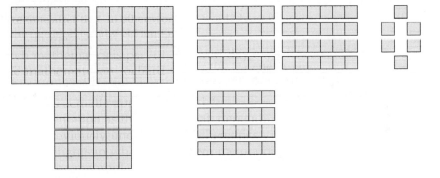

FIGURE 3.5   *Randy's solution*

Ana first adds the hundreds, recording 300 as an intermediate result; next she adds the tens, keeping the answer in her head; she then adds the ones; and finally she adds the partial results (300 + 12 tens + 6) and writes down 426 as the answer. Other students use the conventional algorithm (stacking the addends and then adding the ones, adding the tens and renaming them as hundreds and tens, and finally adding the hundreds) accurately, but some write 3126 as their answer. Becky finds the answer using mental computation and writes nothing down except her answer. When asked to explain, she says, "Well, 2 hundreds and 1 hundred are 3 hundreds, and 5 tens and 5 tens are 10 tens, or another hundred, so that's 4 hundreds. There's still 2 tens left over, and 3 and 3 is 6, so it's 426."

[6] Adapted from NCTM, *Principles and Standards for School Mathematics* (Reston, VA: NCTM, 2000), pp. 86–87.

✖ Whole-Number Addition Algorithms

A teacher observing Mr. Daley's second graders might have a number of questions: Does Ana's or Becky's approach to addition always work? How efficient are these seemingly *alternative* algorithms when compared to the usual standard addition algorithm? Why do some children compute 3126 rather than 426? To gain further insight into these questions and others, we need to look a little deeper into the standard addition algorithm. I'll start off with the usual base-10 notation and then, in order to highlight the structure of the mathematics for you, I'll mirror these results in other bases.

Base-10

Let's return to the problem you and I did earlier on the counting board (and Mr. Daley's students did in class):

$$153$$
$$+273$$

If I did this addition using the standard algorithm, I might explain my answer by noting that I began, much as I did on the counting board, in the ones column, first adding the 3 and the 3, for a sum of 6, and writing down that digit in the ones column. Then I added the 7 and the 5 (actually 70 and 50, respectively) for a sum of 12 (actually 120). Because place value does not allow for the possibility, I cannot put a double digit in a *place,* so I must *carry* the tens digit "1" in this 12 (which is actually 100) to the hundreds column and write the ones digit "2" in this 12 (which is actually 20) in the tens column. Now I add the *carried* 1, the 1, and the 2 (actually 100, 100, and 200, respectively) in the third column for a sum of 4 and write the 4 (which is actually 400) in the hundreds column. The final result, as I have indicated previously, might look something like

^{1}
$$153$$
$$+273 \qquad\qquad (A)$$
$$426$$

   Although my explanation was necessarily tedious (mathematics is multisemiotic and I have limited my explanation to written language[7]), this procedure should be familiar to most adults. However, because it may not be obvious why the procedure works, let's take a deeper look. Remember that we can write any place value number as a linear sum of powers of 10. Thus

$$153 = 1 \cdot 100 + 5 \cdot 10 + 3 \cdot 1$$
$$273 = 2 \cdot 100 + 7 \cdot 10 + 3 \cdot 1$$

-----

[7] Mastering the "pictorial" and "shorthand" aspects of mathematics is crucial to mastering the standard addition algorithm. Note how my presentation is considerably simplified (assuming I am somewhat skilled at using the algorithm) by my use of digits and the plus sign and by my placement and orientation (that is, in specific vertical columns) of the digits of my addends (and the carry).

If I add these, I get

$$153 + 273 = 1 \cdot 100 + 5 \cdot 10 + 3 \cdot 1 + 2 \cdot 100 + 7 \cdot 10 + 3 \cdot 1$$
$$= 1 \cdot 100 + 2 \cdot 100 + 5 \cdot 10 + 7 \cdot 10 + 3 \cdot 1 + 3 \cdot 1$$

and using the distributive property gives

$$153 + 273 = (1 + 2) \cdot 100 + (5 + 7) \cdot 10 + (3 + 3) \cdot 1 \qquad \text{(B)}$$

What is crucial here and in (A) is that powers of 10 are *paired* in each of the addends. It may not be evident to a child why this is important in the standard algorithm—other than because the teacher insists. However, it is clearly not the case that

$$153 + 273 = 1 \cdot 1000 + (5 + 2) \cdot 100 + (7 + 3) \cdot 10 + 3 \cdot 1$$

I add the digits in the ones place

$$153 + 273 = (1 + 2) \cdot 100 + (5 + 7) \cdot 10 + 6 \cdot 1$$

and my next step is to add those in the tens place:

$$153 + 274 = (1 + 2) \cdot 100 + 12 \cdot 10 + 6 \cdot 1 \qquad \text{(C)}$$

If I were to add the digits in the hundreds—and there is nothing wrong with doing that—I would have

$$153 + 274 = 3 \cdot 100 + 12 \cdot 10 + 6 \cdot 1 \qquad \text{(D)}$$

However, the rule is that I cannot have a two-digit number in a *place*. That is, I cannot write

$$153 + 274 = 3126$$

as some of Mr. Daley's students may have (mis)understood. Now

$$12 \cdot 10 = 10 \cdot 10 + 2 \cdot 10 \qquad \text{(E)}$$
$$= \underline{1} \cdot 100 + 2 \cdot 10$$

so

$$153 + 273 = (1 + 2) \cdot 100 + \underline{1} \cdot 100 + 2 \cdot 10 + 6 \cdot 1 \qquad \text{(F)}$$
$$= (1 + 2 + \underline{1}) \cdot 100 + 2 \cdot 10 + 6 \cdot 1 \qquad \text{(G)}$$

If you glance back at my computation in (A), you will see that the "1" I have underlined in (F) and (G) corresponds to the "1" above the digit "1" in 153. Finally, adding the hundreds gives

$$153 + 273 = 4 \cdot 100 + 2 \cdot 10 + 6 \cdot 1 \qquad \text{(H)}$$
$$= 426$$

Reflecting on the work done by students in Mr. Daley's classroom, I note that expression (C) represents Randy's solution and seems to be the juncture at which a number of Mr. Daley's students write 3126 for their final answer. Such missteps seem to result less from difficulties with addition than from a lack of fluency with our base-10 representational system.

The details of my discussion can also be conveniently recorded in vertical notation, using what has been termed the partial-sums method:

$$\begin{array}{r} 100 + 50 + 3 \\ \underline{200 + 70 + 3} \\ 300 + 120 + 6 \end{array}$$

Regrouping gives the sum of 426. Note that both the horizontal additive process I sketched above and the partial-sums method are, in a sense, the usual standard addition algorithm. The seeming difference is that the polished version of the standard addition algorithm, illustrated in (A), employs some shorthand that makes it both more efficient for recording partial sums and simultaneously, for the novice, more opaque.

There are, of course, alternative ways of making sums (partial sums is one). Let's take a look at the methods that Becky and Ana applied. Although the methods Becky and Ana employed may seem unusual, the process of addition that I have sketched above lends itself to describing their solutions. Ana, like many of her classmates, in effect begins with

$$153 + 273 = (1 + 2) \cdot 100 + (5 + 7) \cdot 10 + (3 + 3) \cdot 1 \tag{B}$$

However, she first adds the hundreds:

$$153 + 273 = 3 \cdot 100 + (5 + 7) \cdot 10 + (3 + 3) \cdot 1 \tag{D'}$$
$$= 300 + (5 + 7) \cdot 10 + (3 + 3) \cdot 1$$

then the tens:

$$153 + 274 = 300 + 12 \cdot 10 + (3 + 3) \cdot 1 \tag{E'}$$
$$= 420 + (3 + 3) \cdot 1$$

and finally the ones:

$$153 + 274 = 420 + 6 \cdot 1 \tag{F'}$$
$$= 426$$

As can be seen, this alternative algorithm is certainly valid and, in this instance, somewhat more efficient than the standard addition algorithm. It might be argued that this alternative algorithm requires a greater degree of mental computation and that a child might have difficulty using such an approach with quite large numbers. On the other hand, it might be argued that this alternative algorithm builds a sense of number and is a precursor to estimation.[8]

Becky, in making tens, employs an algorithm that is quite similar to Ana's. She first adds the hundreds:

$$153 + 273 = 3 \cdot 100 + (5 + 7) \cdot 10 + (3 + 3) \cdot 1 \tag{D''}$$
$$= 300 + (5 + 7) \cdot 10 + (3 + 3) \cdot 1$$

---

[8] Think about this for a moment. If I want students to focus on what they are doing—that is, adding numbers—then it might be a good idea to have them focus on the sums they are generating (this is often called estimating). If I begin from the left, I always have the approximate magnitude of the final sum in mind. If I begin from the right, I may have no clue where I'm going to end up.

Then the tens:

$$153 + 273 = 300 + ((5 + 5) + 2) \cdot 10 + (3 + 3) \cdot 1 \qquad \text{(E'')}$$
$$= 300 + 100 + 2 \cdot 10 + (3 + 3) \cdot 1$$
$$= 400 + 2 \cdot 10 + (3 + 3) \cdot 1$$

and finally the ones:

$$153 + 274 = 400 + 2 \cdot 10 + 6 \cdot 1 \qquad \text{(F'')}$$
$$= 426$$

P R O B L E M   3 . 4

Use Ana's or Becky's algorithm to calculate the sum of 2589 + 9852.

Although Ana's or Becky's method may seem awkward to those of us who grew up with the standard algorithms of modern times, it seems not unlikely that such approaches, and others, may have part of the lore of what has been termed "scratch arithmetic."[9] For example, I write the problem as

$$153$$
$$273$$

and then, proceeding from left to right, add the 2 and the 1 for a total of 3, place that 3 below the 2, and scratch out the 1 and 2:

$$\cancel{1}53$$
$$\cancel{2}73$$
$$3$$

I now add the 5 and 7 for a result of 12, place the 2 in the 12 below the 7, and mentally carry the 1 to the next column to the left. I add the 1 and the 3 for a total of 4, place that 4 below the 3, and scratch out the 3, 5, and 7.

$$\cancel{1}\cancel{5}3$$
$$\cancel{2}\cancel{7}3$$
$$\cancel{3}2$$
$$4$$

I now add the 3 and 3 for a total of 6 and, scratching out the 3s, arrive at the sum of 426:

$$\cancel{1}\cancel{5}\cancel{3}$$
$$\cancel{2}\cancel{7}\cancel{3}$$
$$326$$
$$4$$

---

[9] There is evidence for the subtractive version.

Although *making ten* is not an algorithm, it can often, slightly generalized, be used as a heuristic for obtaining a sum. For example, to add 239 and 345, I need only mentally note that

$$39 + 45 = 39 + 1 + 44$$
$$= 40 + 44$$
$$= 84$$

Since $200 + 300$ is 500, mentally summing these partial totals gives

$$239 + 345 = 584$$

P R O B L E M   3 . 5

Use (a) the standard algorithm, (b) *making ten,* and (c) the scratch addition method to compute $29997 + 88$.

Other Bases

Not surprisingly, the standard addition algorithm with minor adjustments can be used to compute sums in any base system. Let's do the sum $111_2 + 101_2$ in base-2 (that is, the sum $7 + 5$ in base-10). All we need to remember is that base-2 is a place value system and that in base-2,

$$0 + 0 = 0$$
$$1 + 0 = 1$$
$$1 + 1 = 10_2$$

Lining things up in the usual manner and applying the standard addition algorithm,[10] we have

$$\begin{array}{r} {\scriptstyle 11} \\ 111_2 \\ +101_2 \\ \hline 1100_2 \end{array} \qquad\qquad \text{(I)}$$

If I were asked to explain what I was doing, I might reply as follows: Well, you start in the ones column. Adding 1 plus 1 gives you 10_2 and because you can't have two digits in a column, you put the 0 in 10_2 down in the ones column and carry the 1 in 10_2 to the twos column. You add this 1 and the 1 and the 0 in the twos column to get 10_2 and, as before, you put the zero in 10_2 down in the twos column and carry the 1 in 10_2 to the fours column. Here you add this 1 and the 1 and the 1 in the fours column. 1 plus 1 gives you 10_2 and adding 1 more gives you 11_2. So you put the rightmost 1 in 11_2 down in the fours column and carry the leftmost 1 in 11_2 to the eights column.

---

[10] When doing such a sum, I would not normally write the subscript indicating the base. However, I have done so in this text to minimize confusion.

Sound peculiar? Let's take a closer look. (Note that I am writing the expansions in base-10, so the leftmost side of my equation will be in base-2 and the rightmost side in base-10.)

$$111_2 = 1 \cdot 4 + 1 \cdot 2 + 1 \cdot 1$$
$$101_2 = 1 \cdot 4 + 0 \cdot 2 + 1 \cdot 1$$

Combining appropriate powers of 2 (that is, lining things up) gives me

$$111_2 + 101_2 = (1 + 1) \cdot 4 + 1 \cdot 2 + (1 + 1) \cdot 1$$

Proceeding from right to left (and, of course, Ana and Becky have shown us that the direction makes no difference), I have

$$111_2 + 101_2 = (1 + 1) \cdot 4 + 1 \cdot 2 + 2 \cdot 1$$
$$= (1 + 1) \cdot 4 + 2 \cdot 2 + 0 \cdot 1$$
$$= (1 + 1) \cdot 4 + 1 \cdot 4 + 0 \cdot 1$$

where I, in essence, carry twice; see (I) above. Finally adding in the fours column, I have

$$111_2 + 101_2 = (1 + 1) \cdot 4 + 1 \cdot 4 + 0 \cdot 2 + 0 \cdot 1$$
$$= 1 \cdot 8 + 1 \cdot 4 + 0 \cdot 2 + 0 \cdot 1$$

or, in base-2: 1100_2 (in base-10 this corresponds, of course, to 12).

Thus, the way one uses the standard algorithm and the justification for its validity are essentially the same in base-2 as in base-10. We could, of course, build a counting tablet that operated in base-2, and in fact, this is typically the way a computer adds. One need only remember three addition facts ($0 + 0 = 0$, $1 + 0 = 1$, and $1 + 1 = 10$) and have a lot of patience.

P R O B L E M   3 . 6

Using the standard algorithm (or, if you wish, Ana's or Becky's alternative method), add $452_6 + 304_6$ in base-6. Check your work by converting to base-10.

✤ Arithmetic Series and Figurate Numbers

The standard addition algorithm can, of course, be easily extended to handle sums of the form

$$
\begin{array}{r}
17 \\
34 \\
51 \\
+68 \\
\hline
\end{array}
$$

However, there are more efficient ways to compute certain sums that arise in any mathematics classroom. Imagine, for example, that your second grade mathematics teacher Ms. Whatzit, in an effort to keep you and your classmates occupied, has written the following problem on the board:

Find the sum of the numbers from 1 to 100.

No fun, right? It is said that when the extraordinary mathematician Karl Friedrich Gauss (1777–1855) was seven years old, his teacher gave his class this very problem. Upon being told that all members of the class were to work the problem independently on their slates and, when finished, put their slates on the teacher's desk, Gauss quickly stood, walked forward, and laid his slate on the teacher's desk. It contained only the correct answer, 5050. When asked how he did the problem, so the story goes, he said he noted that if one writes the numbers from 1 through 50 from left to right and then, below these, writes the numbers 51 through 100 from right to left,

$$1 \quad 2 \quad 3 \quad 4 \ldots \cdots \ldots 47 \quad 48 \quad 49 \quad 50$$
$$100 \quad 99 \quad 98 \quad 97 \ldots \cdots \ldots 54 \quad 53 \quad 52 \quad 51$$

and adds the numbers in each column, the sum is always 101. Hence, because there are 50 such terms, the answer to the sum of the series must be $50 \cdot 101$, or 5050.

This technique for summing up series seems rather powerful. Suppose Gauss's teacher had written this problem on the board:

Find the sum of the odd numbers from 1 to 100.

In this case Gauss might have taken a little longer, but his solution technique works equally well:

$$1 \quad 3 \quad 5 \quad 7 \ldots \cdots \ldots 43 \quad 45 \quad 47 \quad 49$$
$$99 \quad 97 \quad 95 \quad 93 \ldots \cdots \ldots 57 \quad 55 \quad 53 \quad 51$$

The sum of the columns is 100, and because there are 25 terms in the top row, the sum is simply 2500 (or, intriguingly, 50^2). A little more experimentation suggests that for a series of this form—which is called an arithmetic series because there is a constant difference between each term and the one next to it in the series—the sum can be written, more generally, as the function

$$S(n) = n \frac{(a_1 + a_n)}{2}$$

where n is the number of terms in the series, a_1 is the first term, and a_n is the last term.

Let me sketch an induction proof. I'll prove for the arithmetic series denoting the constant difference by d,

$$a_1 \, a_2 \, a_3 \ldots a_n \ldots$$

that

Induction proof

$$S(n) = n \frac{(a_1 + a_n)}{2}$$

for all $n \geq 1$.

Step 1: When there is only one term, $a_1 = a_n$ and, of course, the sum of the series is a_1. On the other hand,

$$S(1) = 1\left(\frac{a_1 + a_1}{2}\right)$$
$$= a_1$$

Step 2: I assume that

$$S(n) = 1\frac{(a_1 + a_n)}{2}$$

for $1 \le n \le N$ and prove that

$$S(N + 1) = (N + 1)\frac{(a_1 + a_{N+1})}{2}$$

Well, I know that

$$S(N + 1) = S(N) + a_{N+1}$$

However, by assumption,

$$S(N) = N\frac{(a_1 + a_N)}{2}$$

so

$$S(N + 1) = N\frac{(a_1 + a_N)}{2} + a_{N+1}$$

I also know that[11]

$$a_2 = d + a_1$$
$$a_3 = d + d + a_1$$
$$\cdots\cdots\cdots\cdots$$
$$a_N = (N - 1)d + a_1$$
$$a_{N+1} = Nd + a_1$$

so

$$S(N + 1) = N\frac{(a_1 + a_N)}{2} + a_{N+1}$$
$$= N\frac{(a_1 + a_N)}{2} + \frac{2a_{N+1}}{2}$$
$$= N\frac{(a_1 + a_N)}{2} + \frac{a_{N+1} + Nd + a_1}{2}$$
$$= \frac{Na_1 + a_1 + Na_N + Nd + a_{N+1}}{2}$$
$$= \frac{(N + 1)a_1 + N(a_N + d) + a_{N+1}}{2}$$
$$= \frac{(N + 1)a_1 + Na_{N+1} + a_{N+1}}{2}$$
$$= (N + 1)\frac{(a_1 + a_{N+1})}{2}$$

as was to be shown.

---

[11] Though somewhat obvious, this may deserve a proof. I'll leave that to you.

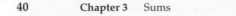

P R O B L E M   3 . 7

What is the sum of the even numbers from 1 to 100?

Determining the sum of the odd numbers had been given a rather nice solution by the Greeks (and the Hindus) as early as 300 BC. One early solution method used figurate numbers. For example, the odd numbers can be pictured as

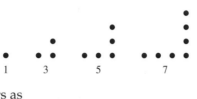

and the square numbers as

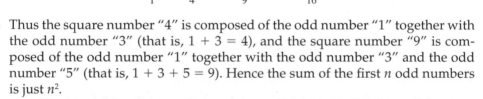

Thus the square number "4" is composed of the odd number "1" together with the odd number "3" (that is, $1 + 3 = 4$), and the square number "9" is composed of the odd number "1" together with the odd number "3" and the odd number "5" (that is, $1 + 3 + 5 = 9$). Hence the sum of the first n odd numbers is just n^2.

The idea of figurate number was generalized by the Greeks, and there are other polygonal numbers (for example, triangular, hexagonal, heptagonal, and octagonal numbers) and their relationships to be explored. Such notions can even be taken into three dimensions. As Archimedes showed, the sum of the squares

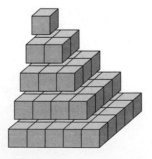

is just the square pyramidal number

$$1^2 + 2^2 + 3^2 + \cdots + n^2 = \frac{1}{6}n(n + 1)(2n + 1)$$

P R O B L E M　　3 . 8

Look up Archimedes' solution on the Internet or take a look at Conway and Guy's *The Book of Numbers* and see how you might pack these blocks together to obtain this result. (*Hint:* Three are easier than one.)

Having seen that the square numbers count the squares, you might wonder what the pyramidal numbers count. Well, the first few are

$$1, 5, 14, 30, 55$$

On the other hand, the number of squares in the 2×2 square is 5 (that is, four 1×1 squares and one 2×2 square), and the number of squares in the 3×3 square

is 14. Thus, I might conjecture, that the nth pyramidal number counts the number of squares in an $n \times n$ square.

P R O B L E M　　3 . 9

Experiment a little further and see what you think.

✂ Indeterminate Problems

We've taken a look at the standard addition algorithm and briefly explored how to sum certain series of integers, so all that is left to consider in this chapter is addition word problems. Many of the additive word problems that students experience in the early grades are of the form

> Yeeman has 22 marbles and Paul gives her 17 more. How many marbles does Yeeman have now?

and involve direct application of the standard addition algorithm. However, by second grade, children are beginning to be exposed to variations such as

> Yeeman has 22 marbles. Paul gives her his marbles and she now has 39 marbles. How many marbles did Paul give Yeeman?

or

> Paul gives Yeeman 17 marbles and she now has 39 marbles. How many marbles did Yeeman have originally?

Because they are still uncomfortable with subtraction, children often solve these latter problems by counting up. That is, a child might say, "Okay, I had 22 marbles and, now that Paul has given me his, I have 39, so I need to count up to 39. One more marble is 23, two more marbles is 24, ..., 17 more marbles is 39. So the answer is 17."

Let's take a look at how this problem might be solved by subtraction. I'll write P for Paul's marbles. Then

$$22 + P = 39$$

or

$$P = 39 - 22$$
$$= 17$$

Note that a crucial step in this solution is isolating the term you wish to determine on one side of the equation, and subtraction performs this task quite nicely. However, suppose Andrew also gives Yeeman his marbles. Does subtraction still work? In this case, our equation takes the form

$$22 + P + A = 39 \tag{J}$$

where A represents Andrew's marbles. Assuming that we are still interested in how many marbles Paul gave Yeeman, I subtract both Yeeman's 22 original marbles and those given by Andrew from both sides:

$$P = 39 - 22 - A \tag{K}$$
$$= 17 - A$$

In this case, the solutions are said to be *indeterminate* and are given by $A = 0$, ..., 17. That is, there are 18 solutions given by the function P—with domain $S = \{0, 1, 2, 3, 4, ..., 16, 17\}$ and codomain the positive natural numbers ($\mathbb{N}$)—such that

$$P(A) = 17 - A$$

I'll now consider a slightly more difficult problem that often appears by third grade and beyond and takes the form

Pencils cost 15 cents and erasers cost 10 cents. If you are to spend exactly $2.00 (forget about tax), what are the different combinations of pencils and erasers that you can buy?

When tackling such problems, students initially employ guess and check; however, many teachers encourage more systematic thinking and may suggest a more tabular approach:

Pencils	Erasers	Total
0	20–200 cents	200 cents
2–30 cents	17–170 cents	200 cents
4–60 cents	14–140 cents	200 cents
6–90 cents	11–110 cents	200 cents
8–120 cents	8–80 cents	200 cents
10–150 cents	5–50 cents	200 cents
12–180 cents	3–20 cents	200 cents

Such a graphical method (a proof by exhaustion, by the way) is significantly more efficient than somewhat random guess and check, but there may
still be some question whether one has provided a complete solution. Around
AD 600, Brahmagupta,[12] using what is now termed linear indeterminate analysis—extensively addressed such concerns. Let's take a look—using current
notation—at how he might have solved this problem. I'm going to let

$$P = \text{the number of pencils}$$

$$E = \text{the number of erasers}$$

Pencils cost 15 cents and erasers cost 10 cents, so I have the equation

$$15 \cdot P + 10 \cdot E = 200$$

Clearly this equation is indeterminate—that is, it has, at least, seven solutions.
I'm going to simplify things a bit by dividing both sides by 5:

$$3 \cdot P + 2 \cdot E = 40 \tag{L}$$

Because the coefficient for the erasers (denoted by E) is smaller than the coefficient for the pencils (denoted by P), I will solve for E. Thus I find, by the same
means as in (K), that

$$2 \cdot E = 40 - 3 \cdot P \tag{M}$$

However, the coefficient of E is not 1, so I divide both sides by 2.

$$E = 20 - (3/2) \cdot P \tag{N}$$

or, after getting rid of my improper fraction,

$$E = 20 - P - (1/2) \cdot P \tag{O}$$

Now I take a crucial step. I know that $(1/2) \cdot P$ must be an integer because
the sum of P, $(1/2) \cdot P$, and E is the whole number 20. Let's call this integer Q.
That is,

$$(1/2) \cdot P = Q$$

or

$$P = 2 \cdot Q$$

Substituting this back in equation (O) gives

$$E = 20 - 3 \cdot Q \tag{P}$$

I claim that equation (P) gives all the possible solutions to the problem. Because
E and P must be positive, Q can take on only the values 0, 1, 2, 3, 4, 5, and 6 (for
example, if $Q = 7$, then $E = -1$). Thus P is 0, 2, 6, 8, 10, or 12 and E is, respectively, 20, 17, 14, 11, 8, or 5. Writing this in functional notation gives

$$P(Q) = 2 \cdot Q$$
$$E(Q) = 20 - 3 \cdot Q$$

---

[12] Oystein Ore, *Number Theory and Its History* (New York: McGraw-Hill, 1948), p. 122.

And both these functions have domain $S = \{0, 1, 2, 3, 4, 5, 6\}$ and codomain $\mathbb{N}$.

More complicated problems yield quite nice solutions with this method. Consider this problem from Mahaviracarya's *Gantia-Sara-Sangraha*:

> Into the bright and refreshing outskirts of a forest, which were full of numerous trees with the branches bent down with the weight of flowers and fruits, trees, such as jambu trees, date-palms, hintala trees, palymyras, punnaga trees and mango trees—filled with many sounds of crowds of parrots and cuckoos found near springs containing lotuses with bees roaming around them—a number of travelers entered with joy.
>
> There are 63 equal heaps of plantain fruits put together and 7 single fruits. These were divided evenly among 23 travelers. Tell me the number of fruits in each heap.

If I let F be the number of plantain fruits in each heap and let T be the fruits allocated to each traveler, then I have the equation

$$63 \cdot F + 7 = 23 \cdot T$$

where F denotes the number of heaps and T the number of fruits received by each traveler.

Applying some persistence and the same approach (*Hint:* 63 is divisible by 7) will yield all solutions. That is,

$$T(Q) = 63Q + 14$$
$$F(Q) = 23Q + 5$$

where the domain of T and F is $\{0\} \cup \mathbb{N}$ and their codomain is $\mathbb{N}$. Note that there are infinitely many solutions, even though these solutions have a particular form.

P R O B L E M   3 . 1 0

What if there are only 7 piles of plantain fruits, 3 single fruits, and 3 travelers? How many fruits are there then in each heap?

Investigations

1. After holiday shopping, a young woman finds that she cannot pay her January rent. She proposes to the landlord that, on each of the (31) days of January that she has not paid her rent, she will give him one of the links of her 18-karat gold necklace, which just happens to have 31 links. Then, at the end of the month, when she pays the delinquent rent, he will return all of the necklace pieces. After duly verifying the quality of the necklace, the landlord agrees.

   But then the woman becomes concerned over the cost of reassembling the necklace at the end of the month. After some thought she has an idea. On the first day, she will cut off one link to give her landlord. But then, on the second day, instead of cutting off another link, she will cut off a pair, give him this 2-link piece, and retrieve the 1 link that he has. Then, on the third day, she will return the single link so that he has the required 3 links, and so on.

The problem is: What is the minimum number of cuts necessary so that on each of the 31 days of January, she can give the landlord the exact number of links required on that day?[13]

2. Let's play around a little with the formula for adding up arithmetic series. In particular, let's consider sums of consecutive counting numbers. Some examples are

$$1 + 2 + 3 = 6 \qquad 7 + 8 + 9 + 10 = 34 \qquad 75 + 76 = 151$$

However, I note that I can't seem to get $2, 4, 8, 16, \ldots, 2^n$ as sums. That is, I don't seem to be able to get a whole-number power of 2 as a sum. Prove that doing so is, indeed, impossible. [*Hint:* Use the formula for the arithmetic series, and keep in mind that if the sum is of the form 2^n, then it is divisible by 2^k for $1 \le k \le n$.]

3. I sold a copy of this text for $50 and then bought it back for $40, thereby clearly making $10 because I had the same book back and $10 besides. Now having bought it for $40, I resold it for $45 and made $5 more, or $15 in all.

When I related this to some friends of mine, one of them, Samantha, immediately spoke up: "Whoa! Wait a minute. You started off with a book worth $50, and at the end of the second sale you had just $55! How could you make more than $5? The selling of the book at $50 is a mere exchange which shows neither profit nor loss, but when you buy it at $40 and sell it at $45, you make $5, and that is all there is to it."

"Nah," said another friend, Derrick. "I claim that when you sell at $50 and buy back at $40, you have clearly and positively made $10, because you have the same book and $10, but when you then sell at $45, you make that mere exchange referred to by Samantha, which shows neither profit nor loss. This does not affect your first profit, so you have made exactly $10."

Unfortunately, none of us is correct. Can you explain why? What information might you add so that I am correct? So that Samantha is correct? So that Derrick is correct? [14]

4. Remember Susie of Chapter 1 and her conjectures? Two somewhat related conjectures are the Goldbach conjecture:

All even numbers can be written as the sum of two primes.

and the Twin Prime conjecture:

There are an infinite number of prime pairs p_1 and p_2 such that $p_1 - p_2 = 2$.

Use Google or some other search engine to trace the history of these conjectures.

---

[13] This problem was related to me by Hyman Bass.
[14] Sam Loyd, *Mathematical Puzzles of Sam Loyd*, ed. Martin Gardner (New York: Dover, 1959).

Differences

The focus of this chapter is on the art of calculating differences—that is, finding solutions to problems of the form

$$5 + x = 9$$

You and I will first examine this art historically and developmentally and then take a closer look at the general-purpose standard subtraction algorithm

$$\begin{array}{r} \overset{1}{\cancel{2}}{}^{1}4 \\ -1\ 6 \\ \hline 8 \end{array}$$

This will be followed by some consideration of what are termed negative numbers. That is, you and I will consider finding solutions to problems of the form

$$24 + ? = 8$$

✢ Subtraction from a Historical Perspective

As with addition, much of what we know about early practices of subtraction comes from speculating on the use of early calculating devices and examining historical judicial and financial accounts. One such account describes a number of the fundamental operations of arithmetic and comes from a passage of the *Fa jing* (a Chinese juristic classic), compiled by Li Kui (424–387 BC):[1]

> A farmer with a family of five cultivates 100 mu of land. Each year one mu produces one and a half of millet, so that the total produce is 150 dan. After deducting one-tenth of this, which is 15 dan, for taxation, there remains 135 dan. Each person consumes one and a half dan per month, so 5 persons consume 90 dan in a year. There is 45 dan left. Each dan is worth 30 qian, so the total worth is 1,350 qian. Subtracting 300 qian for ancestral sacrifices leaves a remainder of 1,050. Each person needs 300 qian for clothing, so the cost for five persons per year is 1,500. There is hence a deficit of 450.

---

[1] Lam Lay Yong and Ang Tian Se, *Fleeting Footsteps: Tracing the Conception of Arithmetic and Algebra in Ancient China* (Singapore: World Scientific, 1992), p. 30.

Such computations were generally not written and were performed, using numerals formed from straight rods (see Figure 4.1), on a flat surface such as a tabletop or mat. However (and intriguingly), it is written in *The Book of Master Laö* that "Those well-versed in calculation use neither counting rods nor texts."[2]

|	||	|||	||||	|||||	T	TT	TTT	TTTT
1	2	3	4	5	6	7	8	9

FIGURE 4.1   *The First Nine Numerals*

It appears that the rods may have been used to perform a calculation such as

$$\begin{array}{r} 24 \\ -16 \\ \hline \end{array}$$

in the following manner: On the counting board, one sets the numerals thusly (the numerals 10 through 40 are as for 1 through 6, but laid horizontally[3]):

with units under units, tens under tens, and so on. Then one commences to subtract from left to right by subtracting 10 from 20, which gives

       that is , $\begin{array}{r} 14 \\ -\ 6 \\ \hline \end{array}$

and then subtracting 6 from 14, which gives 8:

TTT

P R O B L E M   4 . 1

Using some suitable objects—for example, toothpicks—try the following calculations. (a) 47 − 22; (b) 35 − 16; (c) 186 − 97; (d) something daring.

Moving forward to AD 1540, we find in Robert Recorde's *The Ground of Artes* the following characterization of subtraction:[4]

> Subtracting, or rebating, is nothing else but an act to withdraw, or abate, one sum from another that the remainder may appear. Simple problems seem to

[2] Lǐ Yan and Dù Shíràn. *Chinese Mathematics: A Concise History*, trans. John N. Crossley and Anthony Wah-Cheung Lun (Oxford: Clarendon Press, 1987), p. 7.
[3] The numeral 70, for example, is represented by ⊥.
[4] E. R. Sleight, Early English arithmetics. *National Mathematics Magazine*, 16 (1942), 198–215.

be understood readily by the Scholar, but when asked to subtract 5,278,473 from 8,250,003,456, some difficulty arises for the Scholar remarks, "Then I take 7 out of 5, but that I cannot do, what shall I do?"

Master: Mark well what I shall tell you, now, how you shall do in this case. In any figure if the nether sum [the digit in the subtrahend] be greater than the figure of the sum which is over him, then you must put [that is, *add*] 10 to the over figure, and then consider how much it is, and out of that whole sum withdraw the nether figure. But now you must mark another thing also so that when you do put 10 to any figure, you must add 1 still to the figure of the place that followeth in the nether line. So here we have the whole theory of subtraction. But before we go to multiplication I would instruct you to examine your work in subtraction whether it be well done or not [that is, check your work!]. Draw under the lowest number a line, and then add this Remainder, and all the other that you did subtract before, together, and write the result under the lowest line: and if the sum that cometh thereof be equal to the highest of the subtraction then is the subtraction well wrought.

Although this method is still used in other parts of the world, many of us are not familiar with it, so let's see how it might work within the following calculation:

$$\begin{array}{r} 24 \\ -16 \\ \hline \end{array}$$

I cannot subtract 6 from 4 so, according to Recorde, I transform[5] the problem by adding 10 to the 4 (that is, to the 4 in 24), which gives 14:

$$\begin{array}{r} 2\ ^14 \\ -1\ \ 6 \\ \hline 8 \end{array}$$

and then subtract 6 from 14, obtaining 8. I now must add 1 to the 1 (that is, to the 1 in 16):

$$\begin{array}{r} 2\ ^14 \\ -\cancel{1}^2\ 6 \\ \hline 8 \end{array}$$

giving 2. Finally, I subtract 2 from 2, which gives 0, so the difference is 8.

By 1927 there were, in the United States and on the European continent, three general algorithms for subtraction in use: *additions, equal-additions,* and *decomposition* algorithms.[6] The *equal-additions* algorithm is similar to that put forth by Recorde, and the *decomposition* algorithm is essentially the subtraction algorithm we use today. The *additions* algorithm is similar to the equal-additions algorithm although subtraction of, for example, 8 from 14 is envisioned as the solution to

$$6 + x = 14$$

---

[5] Just as in the case of addition, markings to indicate the addition of tens (that $10 + 4$) were not common because such calculations were done mentally.

[6] Much of what follows is taken from Susan Ross and Mary Pratt-Cotter, Subtraction in the United States: A historical perspective, *The Mathematics Educator,* 8(1) (1997), 4–11.

rather than to

$$x = 14 - 6$$

Thus if I were to calculate

$$\begin{array}{r} 24 \\ -16 \\ \hline \end{array}$$

I would proceed as follows:

- Beginning in the units column, I note that the sum of 8 and 6 gives me 14.
- I write 8 in the units column and add the 10 in the 14 to the 10 in the 16 (a variation on this method is to subtract the 10 in the 14 from the 20 in the 26).

$$\begin{array}{r} 2\ 4 \\ -1^2 6 \\ \hline 8 \end{array}$$

- Moving to the tens column, I note that the sum of 2 and 0 gives me 2.
- I then, in effect, write 0 in the tens column.

P R O B L E M   4 . 2

Compute each of the following by using the standard subtraction algorithm and the equal-additions algorithm.

a. 47 − 22

b. 35 − 16

c. 186 − 97

It is interesting to note that in Europe and the United States during the early 1900s, several scholars investigated the relative merits[7] of the equal-additions algorithm and the decomposition, or borrowing, algorithm and found that the equal-additions algorithm was clearly superior. Why didn't it carry the day? Susan Ross and Mary Pratt-Cotter suggest that this may have been primarily due to Brownell's modification (ca. 1937) to the decomposition algorithm, as seen in the now-familiar markup of the present standard subtraction algorithm:[8]

$$\begin{array}{r} 7 \\ 86 \\ -39 \\ \hline 47 \end{array}$$ The child will be allowed to mark through the eight and place seven above it in order to keep track of the borrowing instead of having to remember the process through the entire problem.

✴ Subtraction from a Developmental Perspective

Subtraction proceeds developmentally somewhat as addition. For instance, in computing 9 − 3, children may go from counting a set of blocks to counting the

---

[7] The criteria being speed and accuracy of computation.
[8] Brownell as quoted in Susan Ross and Mary Pratt-Cotter, *Subtraction in the United States.*

subset formed by removing several of these blocks:

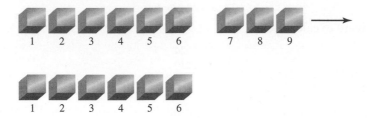

If they are comfortable with notions of cardinality, they may also *count down*

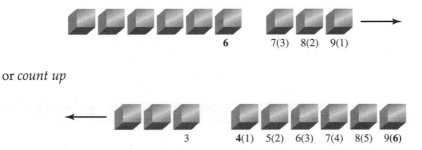

or *count up*

Children have some trouble[9] with *counting down* because one begins, in essence, with the last object counted rather than—as with *counting up*—with the next consecutive object. Such additive tactics (which are, in a sense, the basis of the previously mentioned *additions* subtraction algorithm) are often reinforced through problems of this sort:

$$6 + ? = 14$$

and

> Ornix has picked 6 apples. How may more does he need to pick to have 14?

In U.S. schools, children are consolidating these experiences and committing them to remembrance at the end of second grade and into third grade. Typically, subtraction facts within 5—for example, $5 - 1 = 5$ and $2 - 2 = 0$—are learned first, followed by facts within 10 and then facts within 20. As with addition, children in East Asia take advantage of 10. Here, for example, they make 10 starting from 8:

$$15 - 8 = (10 - 8) + 5$$
$$= 2 + 5$$
$$= 7$$

---

[9] K. C. Fuson, Developing mathematical power in whole number operations. In *A Research Companion to NCTM's Standards*, ed. J. Kilpatrick, W. G. Martin, and D. Schifter (Reston, VA: NCTM, 2003), p. 75.

The inclusion of word problems complicates this state of affairs, as the following vignette[10] illustrates.

Ms. Santi's second grade students had been practicing addition and subtraction fact families and working on problem-solving skills involving both addition and subtraction. While she was out of school for a few days, the substitute teacher, following the district-adopted textbook, has taught students to subtract when the problem asks, "How many more?" Returning to school, Ms. Santi decides to check her students' understanding of this problem type and poses the following problem:

> *Brandon has 14 lollipops. Jeffrey has only 6 lollipops. How many more lollipops does Brandon have?*

The students quickly get to work, using pencil and paper and a variety of manipulatives to solve the problem. While they work, Ms. Santi walks around the room and talks with them about their strategies. To her amazement, many of her students have immediately added the numbers. Susan, for instance, has carefully written

$$\begin{array}{r} {\scriptstyle 1} \\ 1\,4 \\ +\ 6 \\ \hline 2\,0 \end{array}$$

I added 6 and 4 and got 10. Then I carried the 1 and got 20.

Then Brandon speaks up, "I drew all the lollipops too, but I only counted 8. I know the answer is 8." His page just shows a row of 6 lollipops at the top and 14 more scattered below. Melissa says she got 8 too: "I made the numbers with color tiles, and I put them beside each other, and I didn't count the ones that match. I counted 8." Alex, looking at the tiles on Melissa's desk, insists, "You have to count all of them, because you have more than 8." At this point, most of the class begins to discuss whether to count all the lollipops or just some of them. Then Hector shouts excitedly, "I know how to show it! I made it with snap cubes, and I know it's 8 because you put Brandon's and Jeffrey's side by side and you just count the extras!" Hector holds up his snap-cube graph for the class to see.

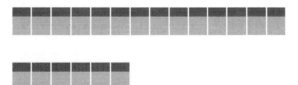

Immediate comprehension sweeps the room and several students repeat, "You just count the extras."

Trying to help her students make a connection with previous textbook subtraction problems, Ms. Santi then asks if they thought subtraction could solve the lollipop problem. No one replies. She then asks them

---

[10] Adapted from C. Barnett-Clarke, A. Ramirez, D. Coggins, and S. Alldredge, *Number Sense and Operations in the Primary Grades* (Portsmouth, NH: Heinemann, 2003).

about the textbook subtraction problems they had completed success-
fully the week before. Heath says, "The substitute teacher said we were
to subtract on those problems." The other students quickly agree. Ms.
Santi writes

$$\begin{array}{r} 14 \\ -\ 6 \\ \hline 8 \end{array}$$

on the board and asks the students how this differs from Hector's snap-
cube solution. Alex says, "The numbers are the same, but you have a minus
sign." There is silence, and then Brandon raises his hand: "When you take-
away, aren't you matching the six with the six in the fourteen? Then the
eight are just the extras."

It is important to keep in mind that these children do not necessarily have
difficulty with subtraction; however, it may be that both the wording of the word
problem (for instance, "How many more . . . ?") and the manipulatives themselves
introduce some ambiguities. Thus, suppose that to simulate the operation of subtraction, I lay down the manipulatives on the table in the usual columnar format

and ask you to demonstrate subtraction using the take-away algorithm. At present
you have 20 items on the table, and no matter how you take away 6, you will still
have 14. What you might do, if you are a thoughtful second grader, is match the 6
in the subtrahend with a six in the minuend and, like Hector, count the extras.

P R O B L E M   4 . 3

Use Hector's method to compute the following, and explain your thinking.

   a. 12 − 5
   b. 15 − 6
   c. 17 − 8
   d. 13 − 7

⚔ Whole-Number Subtraction Algorithms

A teacher observing Ms. Santi's second graders might have a number of questions: Why didn't these children just subtract if they really knew how to do so?
Why didn't Ms. Santi just fix the situation by saying, "When it says 'How many

more?' you just subtract"? How efficient are these and other *alternative* algorithms compared to the usual standard subtraction algorithm? In order to gain further insight into these questions and others, we need to look a little deeper into the standard subtraction algorithm. I'll start off with the usual base-10 notation and then, to highlight the structure of the mathematics, show you how to extend these results to other bases.

Base-10

I'll consider here the standard subtraction algorithm (or decomposition algorithm) and two "alternative"[11] algorithms: the *equal-additions* subtraction algorithm and what I will term a *left-to-right* subtraction algorithm.

Decomposition Algorithm

Consider the following calculation:

$$\begin{array}{r} 1245 \\ -\ 789 \\ \hline 456 \end{array}$$

If I did this subtraction using the standard subtraction algorithm, I might explain my answer by noting that I begin at the right. Because I cannot subtract 9 from 5 (which is not true, by the way), I borrow a 1 from the 4 (actually I borrow a 10 from the 40), making the 5 a 15—note that this breaks the place value rule as I now have 15 ones in the ones place—and subtract 9 from 15 with a difference of 6 and write this in the appropriate column. Now, moving to the next column to the left, I note that I cannot subtract 8 from the remaining 3 (actually 80 from the 30), so I borrow a 1 from the 2 (actually a 100 from the 200), making the 3 a 13 (actually 130), subtract 8 from 13 with a difference of 5 (actually 50), and write this in the appropriate column. Moving to the next column to the left, I note that I cannot subtract 7 from the remaining 1 (actually 700 from 100), so I borrow a 1 from the 1 (actually a 1000 from the 1000), making the 1 an 11 (actually 1100), subtract 7 from 11 with a difference of 4 (actually 400), and write this in the appropriate column. The final result might look something like this if I use the usual markings:

$$\begin{array}{r} 0\ 1\ 3 \\ \not1^1\not2^1\not4^15 \\ -\ \ \ 7\ 8\ 9 \\ \hline 4\ 5\ 6 \end{array}$$

Like the addition algorithm, the standard subtraction algorithm is quite efficient.

---

[11] Remember that whether an algorithm is alternative or not depends on one's perspective. What we know today as the standard algorithm was once an alternative algorithm (and it still is in some parts of the world).

The question we're interested in is "Why does it work?" Let's look.[12] Writing the minuend and subtrahend in terms of powers of 10 gives, respectively,

$$1245 = 1 \cdot 1000 + 2 \cdot 100 + 4 \cdot 10 + 5 \cdot 1$$
$$789 = 7 \cdot 100 + 8 \cdot 10 + 9 \cdot 1$$

Subtracting gives

$$1245 - 789 = 1 \cdot 1000 + 2 \cdot 100 + 4 \cdot 10 + 5 \cdot 1 - (7 \cdot 100 + 8 \cdot 10 + 9 \cdot 1)$$

and rearranging this difference so that it looks like what is going on in the standard subtraction algorithm gives

$$1245 - 78 \ = 1 \cdot 1000 + (2 \cdot 100 - 7 \cdot 100) + (4 \cdot 10 - 8 \cdot 10) + (5 \cdot 1 - 9 \cdot 1)$$

This is the point in the computation where one normally begins to invoke *borrowing*. That is, I cannot take 9 from 5, so I *borrow* a 1 from the 4 in 1245. However, what I actually do is decompose

$$4 \cdot 10 = 3 \cdot 10 + 1 \cdot 10$$

so that

$$1245 - 789 = 1 \cdot 1000 + (2 \cdot 100 - 7 \cdot 100) + (3 \cdot 10 + 10 - 8 \cdot 10) + (5 \cdot 1 - 9 \cdot 1)$$
$$= 1 \cdot 1000 + (2 \cdot 100 - 7 \cdot 100) + (3 \cdot 10 - 8 \cdot 10) + ((10 \cdot 1 + 5 \cdot 1) - 9 \cdot 1)$$
$$= 1 \cdot 1000 + (2 \cdot 100 - 7 \cdot 100) + (3 \cdot 10 - 8 \cdot 10) + (\underline{15} \cdot 1 - 9 \cdot 1)$$
$$= 1 \cdot 1000 + (2 \cdot 100 - 7 \cdot 100) + (3 \cdot 10 - 8 \cdot 10) + 6 \cdot 1$$

Decomposing the $2 \cdot 100$ in like manner gives

$$1245 - 789 = 1 \cdot 1000 + (1 \cdot 100 + 1 \cdot 100 - 7 \cdot 100) + (3 \cdot 10 - 8 \cdot 10) + 6 \cdot 1$$
$$= 1 \cdot 1000 + (1 \cdot 100 - 7 \cdot 100) + (1 \cdot 100 + 3 \cdot 10 - 8 \cdot 10) + 6 \cdot 1$$
$$= 1 \cdot 1000 + (1 \cdot 100 - 7 \cdot 100) + (10 \cdot 10 + 3 \cdot 10 - 8 \cdot 10) + 6 \cdot 1$$

and using the distributive property gives

$$1245 - 789 = 1 \cdot 1000 + (1 \cdot 100 - 7 \cdot 100) + ((10 + 3) \cdot 10 - 8 \cdot 10) + 6 \cdot 1$$
$$= 1 \cdot 1000 + (1 \cdot 100 - 7 \cdot 100) + (\underline{13} \cdot 10 - 8 \cdot 10) + 6 \cdot 1$$
$$= 1 \cdot 1000 + (1 \cdot 100 - 7 \cdot 100) + 5 \cdot 10 + 6 \cdot 1$$

Finally,

$$1245 - 789 = 1 \cdot 1000 + (1 \cdot 100 - 7 \cdot 100) + 5 \cdot 10 + 6 \cdot 1$$
$$= \underline{0} \cdot 1000 + (10 \cdot 100 + 1 \cdot 100 - 7 \cdot 100) + 5 \cdot 10 + 6 \cdot 1$$

---

[12] So that you can observe how the various markings arise out of the mathematics, I have underlined their occurrence.

and, again, using the distributive property gives

$$1245 - 789 = ((10 + 1) \cdot 100 - 7 \cdot 100) + 5 \cdot 10 + 6 \cdot 1$$
$$= \underline{11} \cdot 100 - 7 \cdot 100 + 5 \cdot 10 + 6 \cdot 1$$
$$= 4 \cdot 100 + 5 \cdot 10 + 6 \cdot 1$$
$$= 456$$

Equal-Additions Subtraction Algorithm

Let's take a look at the equal-additions algorithm. Employing markings, the final result might look like this:

$$
\begin{array}{r}
1^1 2^1 4^1 5 \\
- \ \ 7^8\, 8^9\, 9 \\
\hline
4 \ \ 5 \ \ 6
\end{array}
$$

I might explain my answer by noting that I begin at the right. I cannot subtract 9 from 5, so I add 10 to the 5, making the 5 a 15—in the minuend—and subtract 9 from 15 with a difference of 6 and write 6 in the appropriate column and add 10 to the 80 in the subtrahend for a sum of 90. Now, moving to the next column to the left, I note that I cannot subtract the 9 from the 4 (actually the 90 from the 40), so I add 10 (actually 100) to the 4 in the minuend, making it 14, subtract 9 from 14 with a difference of 5 (actually 50), and write this in the appropriate column. Moving to the next column to the left, I add 100 to the 700 in the subtrahend making it 800. I note that I cannot subtract 8 from 2 (actually 800 from 200), so I add 10 to the 2 (actually 1000 to 200), making it 12, subtract 8 from 12 with a difference of 4 (actually 400), and write this in the appropriate column. I then move to the next column, add 1000 to the subtrahend, and subtract the two 1s.

Why does it work? Writing the minuend and subtrahend in terms of powers of 10 gives, respectively,

$$1245 = 1 \cdot 1000 + 2 \cdot 100 + 4 \cdot 10 + 5 \cdot 1$$
$$789 = 7 \cdot 100 + 8 \cdot 10 + 9 \cdot 1$$

Subtracting gives

$$1245 - 789 = 1 \cdot 1000 + 2 \cdot 100 + 4 \cdot 10 + 5 \cdot 1 - (7 \cdot 100 + 8 \cdot 10 + 9 \cdot 1)$$
$$= 1 \cdot 1000 + (2 \cdot 100 - 7 \cdot 100) + (4 \cdot 10 - 8 \cdot 10) + (5 \cdot 1 - 9 \cdot 1)$$

Rearranging this difference so that it looks like what is going on in the equal-additions subtraction algorithm gives[13]

$$1245 - 789 = 1 \cdot 1000 \underline{- 1 \cdot 1000} + 1 \cdot 1000 + 2 \cdot 100 - 7 \cdot 100$$
$$\underline{- 1 \cdot 100} + 1 \cdot 100 + 4 \cdot 10 - 8 \cdot 10 \underline{- 1 \cdot 10} + 1 \cdot 10$$
$$+ 5 \cdot 1 - 9 \cdot 1$$
$$= 1 \cdot 1000 - 1 \cdot 1000 + (1 \cdot 1000 + 2 \cdot 100) - (7 \cdot 100 +$$
$$1 \cdot 100) + (1 \cdot 100 + 4 \cdot 10) - (8 \cdot 10 + 1 \cdot 10) +$$
$$(1 \cdot 10 + 5 \cdot 1) - 9 \cdot 1$$

---

[13] Note that the underlines denote a *borrowing* and a *giving back*. That is, essentially I am adding 0.

Using the distributive property gives

$$1245 - 789 = (12 - 8) \cdot 100 + (14 - 9) \cdot 10 + (15 - 9) \cdot 1$$
$$= 456$$

Left-to-Right Subtraction Algorithm

Both of the subtraction algorithms that we have discussed proceed from the right to the left. There is, however, a subtraction algorithm that proceeds from the left to the right. Consider

$$
\begin{array}{r}
1245 \\
-\ 789
\end{array}
$$

Step 1:
$$
\begin{array}{r}
5 \\
1245 \\
-\ 789
\end{array}
$$
that is, $1200 - 700 = 500$

Step 2:
$$
\begin{array}{r}
4 \\
56 \\
1245 \\
-\ 789
\end{array}
$$
that is, $540 - 80 = 460$

Step 3:
$$
\begin{array}{r}
45 \\
566 \\
1245 \\
-\ 789
\end{array}
$$
that is, $65 - 9 = 56$

Although this algorithm can be found as a component of the galley division algorithm (which will be discussed in Chapter 6), I know of no historical evidence that this algorithm was ever used outside that context.

P R O B L E M   4 . 4

Use left-to-right subtraction and the standard subtraction algorithm to compute (a) $345 - 232$; (b) $345 - 187$. Which is faster and why?

Base-6

Say I was asked to subtract 45_6 from 123_6. If I were to use the standard subtraction algorithm, the resulting calculation might take the form

$$
\begin{array}{r}
0\,1 \\
\mathbf{1}^1\ \mathbf{2}^1\ 3_6 \\
-\quad 4\,5_6 \\
\hline
3\,4_6
\end{array}
$$

I would explain my reasoning, much as in base-10, by noting that I begin at the right. Because I cannot subtract 5 from 3, I borrow a 1 from the 2 (actually I borrow a 6 from 20_6), making the 3 a 13_6 (which is 9 in base-10), subtract

5 from 13_6 with a difference of 4, and write 4 in the appropriate column. Now, moving to the next column to the left, I note that I cannot subtract the 4 from the remaining 1 (actually the 40_6 from the 10_6), so I borrow a 1 from the 1 (actually a 100_6 from the 100_6), making the 1 an 11_6, subtract 4 from 11_6 (actually 7 in base-10) with a difference of 3, and write this in the appropriate column.

Thus the standard subtraction algorithm in base-6 seems structurally like that in base-10. That is not so surprising, because the algorithm works, aside from how we write a number, in exactly the same manner in any base. If I write the minuend and subtrahend, respectively, in terms of powers of 6, I get

$$123_6 = 1 \cdot 36 + 2 \cdot 6 + 3 \cdot 1$$
$$45_6 = 4 \cdot 6 + 5 \cdot 1$$

Subtracting gives

$$123_6 - 45_6 = 1 \cdot 36 + 2 \cdot 6 + 3 \cdot 1 - (4 \cdot 6 + 5 \cdot 1)$$
$$= 1 \cdot 36 + (2 \cdot 6 - 4 \cdot 6) + (3 \cdot 1 - 5 \cdot 1)$$

Rearranging this difference so that it looks like what is going on in the standard subtraction algorithm gives

$$123_6 - 45_6 = 0 \cdot 36 + (6 \cdot 6 + 1 \cdot 6 - 4 \cdot 6) + (1 \cdot 6 + 3 \cdot 1 - 5 \cdot 1)$$
$$= ((6 + 1) \cdot 6 - 4 \cdot 6) + ((6 + 3) \cdot 1 - 5 \cdot 1)$$

Using the distributive property gives

$$123_6 - 45_6 = (7 - 4) \cdot 6 + (9 - 5) \cdot 1$$
$$= 34_6$$

P R O B L E M   4 . 5

Subtract (a) $754_8 - 322_8$; (b) $732_8 - 357_8$.

☆ Negative Numbers

One of the first references to negative numbers is found in China around 100 BC. Here, in *The Nine Chapters on the Mathematical Art* (Jiuzhang Suanshu), negative numbers are used to solve systems of simultaneous equations. In this work, red rods denote positive coefficients and black rods denote negative coefficients. Rules for signed numbers are given.

By the third century, the Greek mathematician Diophantus mentions such numbers in his *Arithmetica*. He notes that, in essence, the equation

$$4x + 20 = 0$$

is absurd, because it would give the solution $x = -5$. By the seventh century, we find rules for using negative numbers in the work of the Indian mathematician/

astronomer Brahmagupta. We also find negative numbers being used to represent debts and positive numbers to represent assets. Nonetheless, even in the twelfth century, the Indian mathematician Bhakasara, while giving negative roots for equations of the form

$$x^2 + x - 20 = 0$$

writes that the negative value is "in this case not to be taken, for it is inadequate; people do not approve of negative roots." Such reluctance persisted, it appears, into the eighteenth century.

Even though some children in the northern climes see negative numbers on the thermometer, one of the first representations many children see is on the number line to the left of zero. Children tend to generalize their counting skills to accommodate negative numbers, but addition and subtraction of such numbers present difficulties. Among the more coherent of such accommodations to signed-number (that is, integer) addition procedures is vector addition on the number line. That is, the leftmost addend is represented as a point on the number line, and the rightmost addend is treated as a displacement according to its sign. Here are two examples:

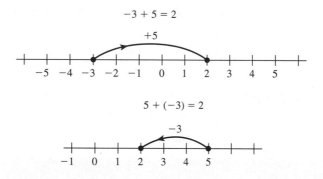

Subtraction, in like manner, can also be modeled by vector differences on the number line. That is, the minuend and the subtrahend are represented as points on the number line, and the displacement is computed from the subtrahend to the minuend and is given the sign of its direction. Thus

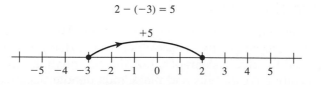

and

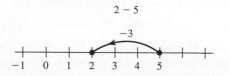

Intriguingly, the source of the difficulties that some students have with negative numbers is inherently mathematical. That is, we have added a group of new numbers to our counting numbers and zero, and we want the entire set of numbers—which we term the *integers*—to have many of the attributes of the counting numbers.

Let's take a deeper look into all this. As I have noted, negative integers essentially arise when we attempt to solve an equation of the form

$$? + 5 = 4$$

or, writing this symbolically, I define the negative integer x to be a solution of the equation

$$x + a = b$$

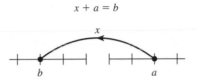

where a and b are positive integers such that $a > b$. In particular, negative integers will be solutions of the equation

$$x + b = 0 \quad (b > 0) \tag{A}$$

For example, -1 will be a solution of the equation

$$x + 1 = 0$$

Positive numbers will be solutions of the equation

$$x = b \quad (b \geq 0) \tag{B}$$

Thus, for example, $+1$ will be a solution of the equation

$$x = 1$$

Given such a definition of *negative integer*, I can use what I know about the counting numbers, $\mathbb{N}$, to compute with negative integers. The rules for negative numbers simply arise from definition (A) and the normal rules for the manipulation of positive numbers and variables.[14]

Sums

Let me demonstrate this. I'll add positive 5 and negative 5. I know the answer is zero, but why? I write

$$x = 5 \qquad \text{(that is, } x = 5\text{)}$$
$$y + 5 = 0 \qquad \text{(that is, } y = -5\text{)}$$

---

[14] These rules are presumed in the following sketch of computation with negative numbers. For further details, see the Appendix.

Thus, if I want to know what the sum of 5 and -5 is, I need to add x and y. When I do this, I get

$$(x + y) + 5 = 5$$

Subtracting 5 from both sides gives

$$(x + y) = 0$$

Thus the sum $x + y$—that is, $5 + (-5)$—must be zero.

How about the sum of positive 7 and negative 5? I know the answer is 2, but let's look at why. As before, I write

$$x = 7 \qquad \text{(that is, } x = 7)$$
$$y + 5 = 0 \qquad \text{(that is, } y = -5)$$

The sum, $x + y$, is

$$(x + y) + 5 = 7$$

Subtracting 5 from both sides gives

$$(x + y) = 2$$

so the sum $x + y$—that is, $7 + (-5)$—must be 2.

On the other hand, note that the sum of negative 7 and positive 5 (that is, -2) is given by

$$(x + y) + 7 = 5$$

Subtracting 5 from both sides gives

$$(x + y) + 2 = 0$$

so the sum $x + y$—that is, $7 + (-5)$—must be -2.

P R O B L E M   4 . 6

Using the number line or the algebraic definition of a negative, compute (a) $-25 + 32$; (b) $-56 + 25$; (c) $45 + (-22)$. Explain your thinking.

Differences

Subtraction is somewhat similar. I'll subtract negative 5 from positive 5 (which I know is 10). Let

$$x = 5 \qquad \text{(that is, } x = 5)$$
$$y + 5 = 0 \qquad \text{(that is, } y = -5)$$

Then the difference is given by

$$x - (y + 5) = 5 - 0$$

or

$$(x - y) - 5 = 5$$

Adding 5 to both sides gives me

$$(x - y) = 10$$

so the difference $x - y$ is 10. In like manner, subtracting positive 5 from negative 5 (which I know is -10) gives me

$$y + 5 - x = 0 - 5$$

and adding 5 to both sides gives

$$(y - x) + 10 = 0$$

so the difference $y - x$ is -10.

P R O B L E M   4 . 7

Using the number line or the algebraic definition of a negative, compute (a) $-25 - 32$; (b) $56 - 25$; (c) $45 - (-22)$. Explain your thinking.

Multiplication

How about multiplication? Why, in fact, does a minus times a minus equal a plus? Let's take a look at positive 7 times negative 5. I know that

$$
\begin{array}{rcl}
7 \times 4 &=& 28 \\
7 \times 3 &=& 21 \\
7 \times 2 &=& 14 \\
7 \times 1 &=& 7 \\
7 \times 0 &=& 0
\end{array}
$$

That is, the right side of these calculations decreases by 7 as the multiplier decreases by 1. If this pattern is to continue, then I would expect that

$$
\begin{array}{rcl}
7 \times -1 &=& -7 \\
7 \times -2 &=& -14 \\
7 \times -3 &=& -21 \\
7 \times -4 &=& -28 \\
7 \times -5 &=& -35
\end{array}
$$

That is, the structure of the positive integers appears to demand that 7 times negative 5 be negative 35.

To show that this is indeed the case, I use my definition of negative number. I have

$$x = 7 \qquad \text{(that is, } x = 7\text{)}$$
$$y + 5 = 0 \qquad \text{(that is, } y = -5\text{)}$$

Multiplying gives

$$x(y + 5) = 7 \cdot 0$$

or

$$xy + 5x = 0$$

Adding $35 - 35$ (that is, 0) to the lefthand side gives

$$xy + 35 - 35 + 5x = 0$$

and factoring out the 5 gives

$$xy + 35 + 5(x - 7) = 0$$

But $x = 7$, so

$$xy + 35 = 0$$

Thus the product xy—that is, $-7 \cdot 5$—is -35.

The result for a minus times a minus is somewhat similar. Let's take a look at negative 7 times negative 5. That is,

$$x + 7 = 0 \qquad \text{(that is, } x = -7\text{)}$$
$$y + 5 = 0 \qquad \text{(that is, } y = -7\text{)}$$

Multiplying gives

$$(x + 7)(y + 5) = 0$$

or

$$xy + 5x + 7y + 35 = 0$$

If we add 35 to both sides, we get

$$xy + 5x + 7y + 35 + 35 = 35$$

or

$$xy + 5(x + 7) + 7(y + 5) = 35$$

However,

$$x + 7 = 0$$
$$y + 5 = 0$$

so

$$xy = 35$$

Thus the product xy—that is, $-7 \cdot -5$—is 35.

A numerical demonstration of this (assuming that one accepts that the product of a negative integer times a positive integer is negative) is as follows. Note that

$$3 \cdot -5 = -15 \qquad 2 \cdot -5 = -10 \qquad 1 \cdot -5 = -5 \qquad 0 \cdot -5 = 0$$

That is, the product increases by 5 every time the multiplier decreases by 1. Hence, I might conjecture that

$$-1 \cdot -5 = 5 \qquad -2 \cdot -5 = 10 \qquad -3 \cdot -5 = 15 \qquad -4 \cdot -5 = 20$$
$$-5 \cdot -5 = 25 \qquad -6 \cdot -5 = 30 \qquad -7 \cdot -5 = 35$$

P R O B L E M   4 . 8

Demonstrate or prove that (a) $8 \cdot (-9) = -72$; (b) $(-5) \cdot (-6) = 30$.

Investigations

1. Three men go to stay at a motel, and the manager charges them $30.00 for a room. They split the cost, paying $10.00 each. Later the manager tells the bellboy that he overcharged the men and that the actual cost should have been $25.00. The manager gives the bellboy $5.00 and tells him to give it to the men.

   The bellboy, however, decides to cheat the men and pockets $2.00, giving each of the men only $1.00. Now each man has paid $9.00 to stay in the room, and 3 × $9.00 = $27.00. The bellboy has pocketed $2.00. $27.00 + $2.00 = $29.00. So where is the missing $1.00?

2. (a) I claim that you can subtract any three-digit number from 1000 by subtracting the hundreds and tens digits from 9 and the units digit from 10. Prove that I am correct.

   (b) I claim that if you pick any two-digit number, add the digits, subtract this sum from the original number, and add the digits of the result, you will always get 9. Prove that I am correct.

3. There is a way of rewriting numbers so that negative and positive integers are written with positive digits. For example, we can write numbers in base -10. The digits are 0, 1, 2, 3, 4, 5, 6, 7, 8, and 9. However, we use a -10 expansion. For example, 10_{10} would be written 190_{-10}:

$$190_{-10} = 1 \cdot (-10)^2 + 9 \cdot (-10)^1 + 0 \cdot (-10)^0$$
$$= 100 - 90$$
$$= 10_{10}$$

   and -10_{10} would be written 10_{-10}:

$$10_{-10} = 1 \cdot (-10)^1 + 0 \cdot (-10)^0$$
$$= -10_{10}$$

(a) Convert 125_{10} to base -10. (b) Convert -125_{10} to base -10. (c) Devise a method for converting any base-10 number to a number in base -10. [*Hint:* For a positive integer n, you might (re)think what Taya is doing in Chapter 2. She gets eleven bundles of 10 and two loose sticks. Now in a -10 expansion, a digit (for example, 7) in the -10s place contributes (for example) -70. Thus that one bundle of 10 is giving us some problems.

However, $10 = 100 - 90$, so $112 = 200 - 90 + 2$. Thus 112_{10} can be written as 292_{-10}.

For a negative integer n, you might think about what happens to the base -10 expansion of $n \cdot (-10)$ when you divide by -10).]

4. A 3×3 magic square is an array such as the following:

where the sum of each horizontal column, the sum of each vertical column, and the sum of each diagonal are all the same.

Jodian is really into magic squares. She decides to make all the 3×3 squares she can using $-2, 4, 10$ down the main diagonal (that is, the diagonal from left to right, top to bottom). (a) How many can she make? (b) Justify your answer. [*Hint:* The common sum of a magic square is always three times the center term. For example, in the magic square shown here, the sum is $3 \cdot 4 = 12$.]

Multiples

The focus of this chapter is on the art of making multiples—that is, finding solutions to problems of the form

$$5 \cdot 6 = ?$$

You and I will first examine this art historically and developmentally and then take a closer look at the general-purpose standard multiplication algorithm, using

as our example. This will be followed by a discussion of prime numbers—for our purposes, positive integers greater than 1 that have only themselves and 1 as factors—and some consequences of the fundamental theorem of arithmetic. That is, every composite number—for our purposes, a positive integer that has integer factors other than itself and 1—can be factored uniquely into prime factors.

❈ Multiplication from a Historical Perspective

In a mathematical sense, multiplication is repeated addition, so the notion probably appeared rather early in human history. However, it was not until about 1650 BC that methods for multiplication began appearing in the historical record. At this time—as shown within problems in the Rhind Papyrus—the Egyptians were using a method for multiplication that required only the doubling of successive numbers and then the addition of the appropriate multiples. Because "doubling" a number written in hieroglyphics could be accomplished by simply rewriting each symbol of the original number (and substituting the next higher unit when this became necessary), multiplication depended only on being able to add. For example,

$$1 \times 142 = 142$$
$$2 \times 142 = 284$$
$$*4 \times 142 = 568$$
$$*8 \times 142 = 1136$$
$$*16 \times 142 = 2272$$
$$16 + 8 + 4 = 28, \text{ so } 28 \cdot 142 = 2272 + 1136 + 568 = 3976$$

A variation of this method can be traced down to the Middle Ages, where it appears in the operation of *duplation and mediation* (or doubling and halving); it is sometimes called Russian multiplication because of its use among Russian peasants. In this method one doubles the multiplicand and halves the multiplier. When halving results in a fraction, the multiplier is rounded down to the nearest whole number, and that step is starred. The multiplicands in starred steps are added to produce the product

$$142 \times 28$$
$$284 \times 14$$
$$568 \times 7*$$
$$1136 \times 3*$$
$$2272 \times 1*$$
$$568 + 1136 + 2272 = 3976$$

The Egyptian method is most easily justified using the binary representation of the numbers (although, of course, such terminology was not used by the Egyptians). For example, as shown in Chapter 2, 28 can be written as

$$28 = 1 \cdot 16 + 1 \cdot 8 + 1 \cdot 4 + 0 \cdot 2 + 0 \cdot 1$$

in base-2. Thus

$$28 \times 142 = (1 \cdot 16 + 1 \cdot 8 + 1 \cdot 4 + 0 \cdot 2 + 0 \cdot 1) \cdot 142$$
$$= 142 \cdot 16 + 142 \cdot 8 + 142 \cdot 4$$
$$= 2272 + 1136 + 568$$
$$= 3976$$

as in the Egyptian method of multiplication. The Russian peasant's method is more easily justified with a little geometry. I can think of the product of 28 and 142 as an area:

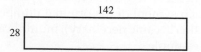

Cutting this rectangle in half gives

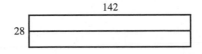

or, with a little rearranging,

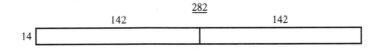

I can do this again and (with the same original area) have

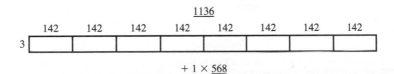

At this point I can't double and halve. However, I can subdivide the 7 as follows:

This gives me the same area as

Now I can again divide up the remaining area and have—after a little arrangement—that

I now am faced with 3 rather than 7, so, preserving the total area as before, I write

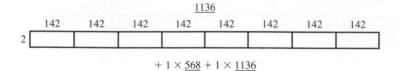

$$+ 1 \times \underline{568} + 1 \times \underline{1136}$$

Dividing this area gives me

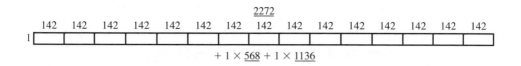

$$+ 1 \times \underline{568} + 1 \times \underline{1136}$$

or

$$1 \times 2272 + 1 \times 568 + 1 \times 1136 = 3976$$

Multiplication was accomplished by the Babylonians (at least as early as 2000 BC) by reference to appropriate multiplication tables, which probably had been compiled by addition. Examples of multiplication as handled by the Greeks are given by a mathematician of the fifth century AD, Eutocius of Ascalon, in his commentary on Archimedes' *The Measurement of the Circle*.[1] Because (as we noted in Chapter 2) the numerals were expressed in alphabetic form, each digit of the multiplier, beginning with the highest, was applied successively to each digit of the multiplicand, also beginning with the highest. The final step was to add these values. Using Hindu-Arabic numerals, such multiplication would look something like this:

```
       142
     × 28
     2000
      800
       40     The sum of the first three terms is 2840.
      800
      320
       16     The sum of the last three terms is 1136.
     3976
```

---

[1] Harold T. Davis, The history of computation. In John K. Baumgart, *Historical Topics for the Mathematical Classroom* (Reston, VA: NCTM, 1969), p. 132.

The basic form is therefore quite similar to ours today, the primary difference being that we write the partial products more compactly.

The Hindu-Arabic system of numbers, with its principle of place value and its zero, began to be seen in Europe near the end of the thirteenth century. Early arithmeticians, recognizing its simplicity, set to work to devise methods for the multiplication of numbers. However, it was really not until the end of the fifteenth century that arithmetic began to assume a somewhat modern form. A book by Nicomachus of Gerasa entitled *Introductio arithmetiea* (around AD 100) provided a multiplication table going as far as 10×10, but it contained no rules for multiplication or division.

The Italians, emulating the Hindus before them, became interested in devising schemes for multiplication and division. Luca Pacioli describes some of these methods in his work *Summa de arithimetica, geometrica, proportioni et proportionolita* (customarily referred to as the *Süma*), which was published in 1494. He lists eight different forms for multiplication, some of them having fanciful names such as *castellucio* ("the method of the little castle") and *graticola* or *gelosia* ("latticcd multiplication"). The latter was so named because it suggested the gratings placed in Venetian windows to protect the dwellers from the gaze of a curious public. Here is an illustration of this scheme of multiplication:

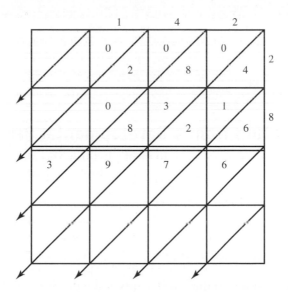

In 2007, a student of mine called my attention to a form of multiplication that was featured on YouTube. YouTube multiplication proceeds, as nearly as I can tell, as follows: One represents the multiplicand by a series of lines running bottom to top and the multiplier by a series of lines running left to right. The different places are set off by gaps.

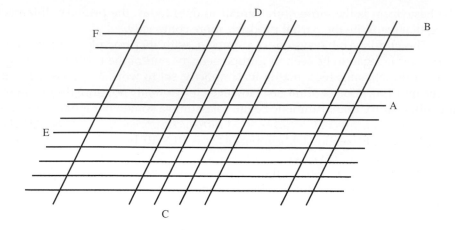

Beginning at A, I note that there are 16 intersections, so I write down 16. At B there are 4 intersections, so I add 16 + 40 = 56. At C there are 32 intersections, so I add 56 + 320 = 376. At D there are 8 intersections, so I add 376 + 800 = 1176. At E there are 8 intersections, so I add 1176 + 800 = 1976. At F there are 2 intersections, so I add 1976 + 2000 = 3976.

P R O B L E M   5 . 1

Multiply 154 × 34 using (a) the Egyptian method, the Russian peasant method; (b) the lattice method.

⚔ Multiplication from a Developmental Perspective

In the United States, students learn to multiply through a stepwise experiential progression of multiplication methods that is similar to that for addition. Initial strategies are repeated addition and skip-counting; for example, counting by 4s gives 4, 8, 12, 16, 20. They often skip-count up and down these lists, using their fingers to keep track and to find different products. They may also use a combination method in which they begin with a product they know and then count on by ones to get to an unknown product. For example, to multiply 5 × 6, they may think, "5 × 5 is 25, and 26, 27, 28, 29, 30 is 5 more." Thus they invent thinking strategies in which they derive unknown products from products they know.[2]

As with addition and subtraction, many of the computational methods developed by students are supported neither by textbooks nor by instruction. Many texts and teachers teach multiplication as an unproblematic memorizing

---

[2] K. C. Fuson, Developing mathematical power in whole number operations. In *A Research Companion to NCTM's Standards*, ed. J. Kilpatrick, W. G. Martin, and D. Schifter (Reston, VA: NCTM, 2003), p. 76.

of isolated facts, often through rote associations. I have seen, for instance, verbal mnemonics such as

> Going fishing, got my bait, six times eight is forty-eight.

Let's take a closer look at these *multiplication facts* by considering the accompanying multiplication table. This is the base-6 system taken up in Chapter 2, and our digits are -, A, B, C, D, E.[3]

X	A	B	C	D	E
A	A	B	C	D	E
B	B	D	A–	AB	AD
C	C	A–	AC	B–	BC
D	D	AB	B–	BD	CB
E	E	AD	BC	CB	DA

Look at the table. I have not listed the *zero facts*, so the table contains 25 facts. Committing this table to memory requires the memorization of 25 facts (committing the usual 10-by-10 multiplication table to memory requires young children to memorize 100 facts—a formidable task. But look more closely at the table, remembering that mathematics has a structure, and see what patterns you can find. You should see a pattern for multiplying A as it corresponds, in its multiplicative properties, to our 1.

- Note that the table is symmetric around the left-to-right diagonal. This symmetry is a consequence of the commutative rule for multiplication.
- C products alternate between C and – in the ones place; the second place to the left (I'll call it the six place) has two A's, two D's, two B's, and so forth. This corresponds to multiplication by 5 in base 10 and the alternation there between 0 and 5.
- In the E pattern, the six place increases by one and the ones place decreases by one; the total of the six digit and ones digits is E. This corresponds to multiplication by 9s in base 10.

---

[3] I could, of course, use 0, 1, 2, 3, 4, 5 instead; however, this alphabetic choice should help you concentrate on the structure of the table.

P R O B L E M   5 . 2

Describe the pattern in the B row.

Approaching the learning of multiplication as pattern finding both scaffolds and simplifies the task. In a fundamental way, mathematics *is* the studying and using of such patterns. Note that it is not that memorization is unimportant—the student must still recognize relevant patterns—but understanding the structure of a 10×10 base-10 multiplication table may open up possibilities within and without a 10×10 table.[4]

P R O B L E M   5 . 3

Create a multiplication table for a base-7 place value system.

Even after they have identified patterns, students still need much experience so that they will be able to compute individual products rapidly. As students consolidate such skills, there is, in U.S. classrooms, a move to multidigit multiplication. This may involve[5] a degree of scaffolding:

1. Direct modeling with objects or drawings (by ones and by tens and ones), to
2. Written methods involving repeatedly adding (sometimes by repeated doubling, a surprisingly effective method used historically), to
3. Partitioning methods,[6] to
4. The standard multiplication algorithm.

In more traditional classrooms, there is often little scaffolding, and students move directly from memorizing the "times table" to practicing application of the standard multiplication algorithm.

✳ Whole-Number Multiplication Algorithms

Knowledge of multiplication by 10 and understanding the distributive rule are essential to understanding multidigit multiplication. The distributive rule states that

$$a(b + c) = ab + ac$$

---

[4] For instance, the commutative rule is valid in a table of any size.
[5] Fuson, pp. 84–85.
[6] Examples of partitioning methods include partitioning either the multiplier or multiplicand into tens and ones, partitioning both multiplier and multiplicand into tens and ones, partitioning using numbers other than ten.

That is, multiplication distributes over addition. For example,

$$2\,(22) = 2(20 + 2)$$
$$= 2\,(20) + 2(2)$$
$$= 40 + 4$$
$$= 44$$

Multiplication by 10 (or 100, 1000, etc.) builds on the structure of the base-10 number system. I can write the number 342 as

1000	100	10	1
	3	4	2

where its place in this table indicates its place value. If I multiply 342 by 10, it simply shifts to the left:

1000	100	10	1
3	4	2	

leaving, in effect, zero in the units positions. Thus $10 \times 342 = 3420$. I can also demonstrate this feature of our base 10 system by writing 342 in expanded notation:

$$342 = 3 \cdot 10^2 + 4 \cdot 10^1 + 2 \cdot 10^0$$

so

$$10 \times 342 = 10\,(3 \cdot 10^2 + 4 \cdot 10^1 + 2 \cdot 10^0)$$
$$= 3 \cdot 10^3 + 4 \cdot 10^2 + 2 \cdot 10^1$$
$$= 3420$$

Putting all these the key components together, you and I are ready to examine how multidigit multiplication works. I'll consider 28×142 and write both in expanded notation. Thus

$$28 \times 142 = (2 \cdot 10^1 + 8)\,(1 \cdot 10^2 + 4 \cdot 10^1 + 2)$$

Using the distributive rule gives

$$28 \times 142 = (2 \cdot 10^1)\,(1 \cdot 10^2 + 4 \cdot 10^1 + 2) + (8)\,(1 \cdot 10^2 + 4 \cdot 10^1 + 2)$$
$$= (2 \cdot 10^1)\,(1 \cdot 10^2 + 4 \cdot 10^1 + 2) + (8 \cdot 10^2 + 32 \cdot 10^1 + 16) \qquad \text{(A)}$$

Note that $8 \cdot 10^2 + 32 \cdot 10^1 + 16$ is not a proper base-10 number and that to make it such, we must regroup and, in essence, *carry*:

$$8 \cdot 10^2 + 32 \cdot 10^1 + 16 = 8 \cdot 10^2 + \underline{3 \cdot 10^2} + 2 \cdot 10^1 + \underline{1 \cdot 10^1} + 6 \qquad \text{(B)}$$
$$= 11 \cdot 10^2 + 3 \cdot 10^1 + 6$$
$$= 1 \cdot 10^3 + 1 \cdot 10^2 + 3 \cdot 10^1 + 6$$
$$= 1136$$

Thus

$$28 \times 142 = (2 \cdot 10^1)(1 \cdot 10^2 + 4 \cdot 10^1 + 2) + 1136 \qquad \text{(C)}$$
$$= (10^1)(2 \cdot 10^2 + 8 \cdot 10^1 + 4) + 1136$$
$$= (10^1)(284) + 1136$$

Using the fact that multiplication by 10 shifts the number one place to the left gives

$$28 \times 142 = 2840 + 1136 = 3976 \qquad \text{(D)}$$

Take a look at the standard algorithm:

$$
\begin{array}{r}
3\,1 \\
142 \\
\times\ 28 \\
\hline
1136 \\
2840 \\
\hline
3976
\end{array}
$$

Can you see where the various parts come from? The first and second rows arise simply from the distributive property and the fact that I decomposed the multiplier and multiplicand with respect to place value. The carries (1 and 3) arise from the necessity to write numbers properly in our base-10 system, and the 0 in 2480 arises from multiplication by 10. That shift becomes even more evident when I write the standard algorithm in its most efficient form[7] as

$$
\begin{array}{r}
142 \\
\times\ 28 \\
\hline
1136 \\
284 \\
\hline
3976
\end{array}
$$

Obvious isn't it. Now I'll give it a try with our base-6 system. Consider

$$ABC \times BE$$

Using the standard multiplication algorithm, I have

$$
\begin{array}{r}
AA \\
ABB \\
\times\ BE \\
\hline
A\text{-}E\ D \\
BDD\text{-} \\
\hline
CECD
\end{array}
$$

---

[7] And its most opaque form.

Here is an explanation: Starting at the right and moving left,[8] I first compute E × B. This, from the multiplication table, is AD. Thus I put down D and carry A. Now E × B is AD, so I add the A that I carried to AD, which, of course, gives me AE. Thus I put down the E and carry the second A. Then I multiply E times A, which gives me E, and I add the second A, which gives me A-, and I put this down. My first row now reads A-ED.

I compute the second line much as I did the first, remembering that I must shift because I will be multiplying by B (the B in BE), which is in the sixes place (I'll denote that shift with '–' although strictly speaking that is not necessary). First I compute B × B, which is D, and write that down. Then I compute B × B, which is D, and write that down. Finally, I compute B times A, which is B, and write that down. I now have BDD- in the second row. Finally, I add my two partial products to get CECD.

P R O B L E M   5 . 4

Multiply (a) CBA by AAA; (b) CBA by CD.

✷ Prime Numbers and Factoring

In this section, you and I will briefly review some characteristics of primes and then, because factorization is a part of the elementary mathematics curriculum, we will examine prime factorizations.

Prime Numbers

An integer $p > 1$ is called a prime number when its only divisors are ± 1 and $\pm p$. The primes below 100 are

2	13	31	53	73
3	17	37	59	79
5	19	41	61	83
7	23	43	67	89
11	29	47	71	97

The number 2 is the only even prime. A number $m > 1$ that is not a prime is called composite. The first few composite numbers are

4	6	8	9	10	12	14	15	16	18	20

---

[8] You might wonder whether there is a reasonably efficient left-to-right version. The answer is, of course, "Yes." However, I have never seen one in the historical record. Okay, how about this?

$$\begin{array}{r} 142 \\ 28 \\ \underline{284} \\ 3666 \\ 97 \end{array}$$

In an analogously fashion I could introduce the negative prime numbers −2, −3, −5, . . . and the negative composite numbers −4, −6, ... However, in the following discussion of factors of numbers, I shall consider only the positive primes.

There is an ancient method of finding the primes known as the sieve of Eratosthenes.[9] Eratosthenes' sieve consists in writing down all numbers up to some limit, say 100:

1 2 3 ~~4~~ 5 ~~6~~ 7 ~~8~~ ~~9~~ ~~10~~ 11 ~~12~~ 13 ~~14~~ ~~15~~ ~~16~~ 17 ~~18~~ 19 ~~20~~
~~21~~ ~~22~~ 23 ~~24~~ ~~25~~ ~~26~~ ~~27~~ ~~28~~ 29 ~~30~~ 31 ~~32~~ ~~33~~ ~~34~~ ~~35~~ ~~36~~ 37 ~~38~~ ~~39~~ ~~40~~
41 ~~42~~ 43 ~~44~~ ~~45~~ ~~46~~ 47 ~~48~~ ~~49~~ ~~50~~ ~~51~~ ~~52~~ 53 ~~54~~ ~~55~~ ~~56~~ ~~57~~ ~~58~~ 59 ~~60~~
61 ~~62~~ ~~63~~ ~~64~~ ~~65~~ ~~66~~ 67 ~~68~~ ~~69~~ ~~70~~ 71 ~~72~~ 73 ~~74~~ ~~75~~ ~~76~~ ~~77~~ ~~78~~ 79 ~~80~~
~~81~~ ~~82~~ 83 ~~84~~ ~~85~~ ~~86~~ ~~87~~ ~~88~~ 89 ~~90~~ ~~91~~ ~~92~~ ~~93~~ ~~94~~ ~~95~~ ~~96~~ 97 ~~98~~ ~~99~~ ~~100~~

From this series I first, skip-counting from 2, strike out every second number— that is, the numbers 4, 6, 8 . . . . Counting from the first remaining number, 3, every third number (that is, 6, 9, 12, . . .) is marked; some of them will thus be marked twice. The next remaining number is 5, which is a prime because it has not been struck out as divisible by 2 or 3; then every fifth number (10, 15, 20, . . .) is eliminated. The first remaining number, 7, is a prime because it is not divisible by 2, 3, or 5, and its multiples (14, 21, . . .) are eliminated. In this manner, all primes between 1 and 100 may be determined successively.

Eratosthenes' sieve is, at best, tedious; however, the following observation makes it a little less so. In the preceding example, when all multiples of 7 have been marked in the fourth step, the remaining unmarked numbers will now include all primes below 100, because no remaining number N has any factor less than the next prime $11 > \sqrt{N}$. Thus, for example, when checking whether 329 is prime, I need only check factors up to 17, because $17 < \sqrt{329}$ and $19 > \sqrt{329}$.

P R O B L E M   5 . 5

Determine (a) whether 241 is prime; (b) whether 341 is prime. Show your work.

___

There are other less systematic methods for generating primes. I will illustrate one that Euclid used around 300 BC. Let $Q = \{p_1, p_2, \ldots, p_n\}$ be any set of prime numbers. I take their product

$$P = p_1 \cdot p_2 \cdots p_n$$

and add 1. Then $P + 1$ is certainly either a prime or not a prime. If it is a prime, I now have a prime p other than those in the set Q. If it is not, it must be divisible by some prime p. But p cannot be identical with any of the primes in Q, because then it would simultaneously divide P, $P + 1$, and hence their difference, which is 1. This is impossible. Therefore, in any case, I have generated a prime not in Q.

___

[9] Eratosthenes (276–194 BC) was a Greek scholar and chief librarian of the famous library in Alexandria. He is noted for his chronology of ancient history and for his measurement of the meridian between Assuan and Alexandria, which made it possible to estimate the size of the earth with remarkable accuracy.

For instance, I have

$2 \cdot 3 + 1 = 7$ (7 is a prime)

$2 \cdot 3 \cdot 5 + 1 = 31$ (31 is a prime)

$2 \cdot 3 \cdot 5 \cdot 7 + 1 = 211$ (211 is a prime)

$2 \cdot 3 \cdot 5 \cdot 7 \cdot 11 + 1 = 2311$ (2311 is a prime)

$2 \cdot 3 \cdot 5 \cdot 7 \cdot 11 \cdot 13 + 1 = 30{,}031 = 59 \cdot 509$ (59 and 509 are primes)

$2 \cdot 3 \cdot 5 \cdot 7 \cdot 11 \cdot 13 \cdot 17 + 1 = 510{,}511 = 19 \cdot 97 \cdot 277$ (19, 97, and 277 are primes)

$2 \cdot 3 \cdot 5 \cdot 7 \cdot 11 \cdot 13 \cdot 17 \cdot 19 + 1 = 9{,}699{,}691 = 347 \cdot 27{,}953$ (347 and 27,953 are primes)

Just how many primes are there, anyway? One of the first known proofs that there are an infinitude of primes was given, around 300 BC, by Euclid in his *Elements* (Proposition 20, Book IX).

Proof: This will be a proof by contradiction. I assume, to the contrary, that there are a finite number of primes. That is, $Q = \{p_1, p_2, \ldots, p_n\}$. However, in this case, as I have just shown, I can generate a prime p not in Q. This is a contradiction. Hence there are infinitely many primes.

> Proof by contradiction

However, although there are infinitude of primes, they tend to thin out (see Figures 5.1, 5.2, and 5.3).

0+	1–100	100–200	200–300	300–400	400–500	500–600	600–700	700–800	800–900	900–1000
	25	21	16	16	17	14	16	14	15	14

FIGURE 5.1 *Numbers of Primes from 1 to 1000*

1,000,000+	1–100	100–200	200–300	300–400	400–500	500–600	600–700	700–800	800–900	900–1000
	6	10	8	8	7	7	10	5	6	8

FIGURE 5.2 *Numbers of Primes from 1,000,000` to 1,001,000*

10,000,000+	1–100	100–200	200–300	300–400	400–500	500–600	600–700	700–800	800–900	900–1000
	2	6	6	6	5	4	7	10	9	6

FIGURE 5.3 *Numbers of Primes from 10,000,000 to 10,001,000*

The Prime Number theorem states that for large values of x, the number of primes less than or equal to x, $\pi(x)$, is approximately given by

$$\pi(x) \sim \frac{x}{\ln x}$$

where $\ln x$ indicates the natural logarithm of x.

Prime Factorizations

Around the fourth or fifth grade, children begin to spend some time factoring numbers. For example, the number 30 factors as follows:

That is, $30 = 2 \cdot 3 \cdot 5$. In fact, by the Fundamental Theorem of Arithmetic,[10] every composite number N can be factored uniquely into prime factors:[11]

$$N = p_1^{a_1} p_2^{a_2} \cdots p_r^{a_r}$$

where the p_i's are the various prime factors and a_i is the multiplicity—that is, the number of times p_i occurs in the prime factorization. Thus $60 = 2^2 \cdot 3 \cdot 5$.

P R O B L E M   5 . 6

Give prime factorizations for (a) 3600 and (b) 621.

Because $60 = 2^2 \cdot 3 \cdot 5$, I know that some factors of 60 are 60 and 1, 2, 4, 6, 15, etc. An interesting mathematical question is whether, given a particular number, we can determine how many factors it has and whether we can easily create a list of factors. It turns out that the number of factors of N, where

$$N = p_1^{a_1} p_2^{a_2} \cdots p_r^{a_r}$$

is a prime factorization in terms of primes $p_1, p_2, \ldots, p_r$, is given by

$$v(N) = (a_1 + 1)(a_2 + 1) \cdots (a_r + 1)$$

Proof: Now for any i,

$$p_i^0 = 1$$

so any factor g of N can be written in the form[12]

$$g = p_1^{b_1} p_2^{b_2} \cdots p_r^{b_r}$$

where $0 \le b_i \le a_i$ for all i. Thus, as I construct factors of N, I can choose the multiplicity of p_1 to be $0, 1, \ldots, a_1$; that is, I can choose the multiplicity for p_1 in $a_1 + 1$ ways. In similar fashion, I can choose the multiplicity of p_2 in $1 + a_2$ ways, and so on. Thus the number of factors of a number—much as in a combinatorial situation involving pants, shirts, and shoes—is

$$v(N) = (a_1 + 1)(a_2 + 1) \cdots (a_r + 1)$$

---

[10] See the Appendix for a proof.
[11] This theorem is called the Prime Factorization theorem. I will assume it in the discussion that follows.
[12] Think about this for a moment, and note that for $0 \le b_i \le a_i$, $p_i^{a_i}$ is divisible by $p_i^{b_i}$.

For example,

$$v(60) = (2 + 1)(1 + 1)(1 + 1) = 12$$

and hence 60 has 12 factors. They are[13]

$1 \times 1 \times 1 = 1$	$2 \times 1 \times 1 = 2$	$4 \times 1 \times 1 = 4$
$1 \times 1 \times 5 = 5$	$2 \times 1 \times 5 = 10$	$4 \times 1 \times 5 = 20$
$1 \times 3 \times 1 = 3$	$2 \times 3 \times 1 = 6$	$4 \times 3 \times 1 = 12$
$1 \times 3 \times 5 = 15$	$2 \times 3 \times 5 = 30$	$4 \times 3 \times 5 = 60$

P R O B L E M   5 . 7

Compute $v(3600)$ and $v(621)$. List the factors of 621.

Investigations

1. Historically, cryptography depended on a secret key that two or more parties used to decrypt information encrypted by a mutually agreed-upon method. One of the encryption algorithms in common use today is public key cryptography. The security of this technique is a consequence of the difficulty of finding two prime factors of a very large number. Give an example of how this algorithm works, and trace its history.

2. A *perfect number* is a number that is the sum of its aliquot divisors (that is, all divisors, including 1, other than itself). For example, 6 and 28 are perfect numbers because $6 = 1 + 2 + 3$ and $28 = 1 + 2 + 4 + 7 + 14 = 28$. Prove that a number of the form

$$P = 2^{p-1}(2^p - 1) \qquad (p > 1)$$

is perfect if $q = 2^p - 1$ is a prime. [*Hint:* It may help to consider the product

$$\sigma(N) = (1 + p_1 + p_1^2 + \cdots + p_1^{a_1})(1 + p_2 + p_2^2 + \cdots + p_1^{a_2}) \cdots$$
$$(1 + p_r + p_r^2 + \cdots + p_r^{a_r}) \tag{E}$$

where N has the prime factorization

$$N = p_1^{a_1} p_2^{a_2} \cdots p_r^{a_r}$$

Because all factors of N (including N itself) appear in the expansion of $\sigma(N)$, $\sigma(N)$ is the sum of the factors of N, and hence, if $\sigma(N) = 2N$, then N is a perfect number.

---

[13] Review, if necessary, the material in Chapter 2 on creating an outfit given a certain number of pants, shoes, and shirts.

You might want to experiment with this expansion a bit. For example, look at the expansion of $\sigma(60)$:

$$\sigma(60) = (1 + 2 + 4)(1 + 3)(1 + 5)$$
$$= (1 + 2 + 4)\,(1 \times 1 + 1 \times 3 + 1 \times 5 + 3 \times 5)$$
$$= 1 \times 1 \times 1 + 1 \times 1 \times 3 + 1 \times 1 \times 5 + 1 \times 3 \times 5 + 2$$
$$\times 1 \times 1 + 2 \times 1 \times 3 + 2 \times 1 \times 5 + 2 \times 3 \times 5 + 4 \times 1$$
$$\times 1 + 4 \times 1 \times 3 + 4 \times 1 \times 5 + 4 \times 3 \times 5$$

and compare the expansion with the list of factors given previously.]

3. A prime of the form $2^p - 1$ is called a Mersenne prime. Outline the intriguing history of Mersenne primes from their discovery to present times.

4. (a) What digits may appear as the last digit of a square number? (b) As the last digit of a cube? Justify your answers. [*Hint:* We can (refer to the form of the base-10 expansion) write any positive integer as $10a + b$, where $0 \le b \le 9$.]

5. Two numbers N and M are said to be relatively prime if the only factor they have in common is 1. In 1760 Leonard Euler posed the following question:

When N is some integer, how many of the numbers 1, 2, 3, ..., $N - 1$, N are relatively prime to N?

and gave a solution. This number, $\varphi(N)$, is usually denoted by φ and is known as Euler's φ-function. I have, for the first few integers,

$$\varphi(2) = 1 \qquad \{1\}$$
$$\varphi(3) = 2 \qquad \{1, 2\}$$
$$\varphi(4) = 2 \qquad \{1, 3\}$$
$$\varphi(5) = 4 \qquad \{1, 2, 3, 4\}$$

In particular, Euler showed that if

$$N = p_1^{a_1} p_2^{a_2} \cdots p_r^{a_r}$$

then

$$\varphi(N) = N\left(1 - \frac{1}{p_1}\right)\left(1 - \frac{1}{p_2}\right) \cdots \left(1 - \frac{1}{p_r}\right)$$

Find a suitable text that gives a proof, or surf the Internet and, as you read the proof, write your own proof for this result. This, by the way, is one of the few effective ways to read a mathematics text.

6. Demonstrate why YouTube multiplication works.

Divisibility and Remainders

This chapter focuses on the art of division. You and I will first examine this art historically and developmentally and then take a closer look at the general-purpose standard long-division algorithm, as illustrated by

$$
\begin{array}{r}
124 \\
16)\overline{1987} \\
\underline{16} \\
38 \\
\underline{32} \\
67 \\
\underline{64} \\
3
\end{array}
$$

This will be followed by a discussion of clocks, congruences, and divisibility rules. For example, we know, without performing any division, that any number that ends in a multiple of 2 is divisible by 2. However, could we know that 4576890345789 is divisible by 3, 9, or possibly 7 without performing long division?

✄ Division from a Historical Perspective

As I noted earlier, one source of our knowledge of the historical roots of arithmetic is the Rhind Papyrus (more accurately called the Ahmes Papyrus). Here we find the problem "divide 19 by 8" (or "calculate with 8 until you find 19"). The solution to the problem, in modern notation, proceeds as follows:

$$1 \times 8 = 8$$

$$2 \times 8 = 16*$$

$$\frac{1}{2} \times 8 = 4$$

$$\frac{1}{4} \times 8 = 2*$$

$$\frac{1}{8} \times 8 = 1*$$

The asterisked items in the righthand column add to 19, so the solution is just

$$19 \div 8 = 2 + \frac{1}{4} + \frac{1}{8}$$

Note that, in essence, I use doubling to determine the quotient and halving to determine the remainder.

A somewhat more complex example is 1987 divided by 16. Here I need to calculate with 16 until I find 1987:

$$1 \times 16 = 16$$
$$2 \times 16 = 32$$
$$4 \times 16 = 64*$$
$$8 \times 16 = 128*$$
$$16 \times 16 = 256*$$
$$32 \times 16 = 516*$$
$$64 \times 16 = 1032*$$

The asterisked items thus far get me up to 1984 (that is, 124×16). I need 3 more.

$$\frac{1}{2} \times 16 = 8$$
$$\frac{1}{4} \times 16 = 4$$
$$\frac{1}{8} \times 16 = 2*$$
$$\frac{1}{16} \times 16 = 1*$$

So my solution is

$$1789 \div 16 = 124 + \frac{1}{8} + \frac{1}{16}$$

P R O B L E M   6 . 1

Divide 273 by 8 using the Egyptian method.

The Greek method for division is somewhat similar to the Egyptian method. However, from approximately AD 895 to approximately AD 1600 a "scratch" method of division, possibly of Hindu origin, was the most widely used form of division[1] (it is still used in parts of North Africa). For example, I proceed as follows to divide 1897 by 16. I begin by writing the problem as[2]

$$1987 \qquad ($$
$$16$$

As usual I look for a trial multiplier—1 works—and write

$$1987 \qquad (1$$
$$16$$

[1] NCTM.
[2] If, for example, my divisor were 26, I would indent it one space to the right.

I then mentally multiply the trial multiplier by the divisor and, in essence, use the scratch method of subtraction to compute the difference $(1 - 1 \cdot 1 = 0$ and $9 - 1 \cdot 6 = 3)$

$$
\begin{array}{l}
03 \\
\cancel{1}987 \quad\quad (1 \\
\cancel{16}
\end{array}
$$

Then, indenting one space to the right, I rewrite the divisor

$$
\begin{array}{l}
03 \\
\cancel{1}987 \quad\quad (1 \\
\cancel{1}66 \\
1
\end{array}
$$

and look for a trial multiple of 16, which gets me near to 38. This happens to be 2. I mentally multiply the divisor by 2, and using, in essence, the scratch method of subtraction to compute the difference, I have $(3 - 2 \cdot 1 = 1)$

$$
\begin{array}{l}
\text{l} \\
0\cancel{3} \\
\cancel{1}987 \quad\quad (12 \\
\cancel{1}66 \\
1
\end{array}
$$

and $(18 - 2 \cdot 6 = 6)$

$$
\begin{array}{l}
0 \\
\cancel{1} \\
0\cancel{36} \\
\cancel{1}987 \quad\quad (12 \\
\cancel{1}66 \\
\cancel{1}
\end{array}
$$

Then, indenting one space to the right, I rewrite the divisor

$$
\begin{array}{l}
0 \\
\cancel{1} \\
0\cancel{36} \\
\cancel{1}987 \quad\quad (12 \\
\cancel{1}666 \\
\cancel{1}1
\end{array}
$$

and look for a trial multiple of 16 that gets me near to 67. This happens to be 4. I mentally multiply the divisor by 4, and using, in essence, the scratch method of subtraction to compute the difference, I have $(6 \quad 4 \cdot 1 - 2)$

0
~~1~~2
0~~36~~
~~1987~~ (124
~~1666~~
~~11~~

and $(27 - 4 \cdot 6 = 3)$

00
~~12~~
0~~36~~3
~~1987~~ (124 (A)
~~1666~~
~~11~~

My final answer is 124 with remainder 3.

Because the figure in (A) apparently resembles a galley, this was termed the *galley* method. The galley method is reputed to be faster than modern long division and is thought to have fallen out of use for want of "canceled types" in printing (that is, type of the form ~~1~~). A somewhat more complicated problem and its solution appear in *Holder's Arithmetic,* which was printed in Boston in 1719:[3]

8
~~97~~5
~~9863~~0
~~987529~~3
~~98764181~~0
~~98765206098~~
~~987654195987~~6
~~49382714848765~~4
~~246913578637654 3~~2
~~12345678998765432 1~~ (124999999
~~98765432111111111~~
~~987654322222222~~
~~9876543333333~~
~~98765444444~~
~~987655555~~
~~9876666~~
~~98777~~
~~988~~
~~9~~

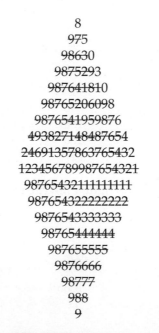

FIGURE 6.1 ***12345678998765432 1 Divided by 987654321***

---

[3]Louis Charles Karpinski, *The History of Arithmetic* (Chicago: Rand McNally, 1925), p. 119.

P R O B L E M   6 . 2

Divide 7890 by 33 using the galley method.

Calandari's arithmetic book of 1491 was the first to use what we now term the standard algorithm for division. Robert Recorde illustrates this algorithm in his *The Grounde of Artes* (1542), dividing 7890 by 33:

$$33) 7890 (239 \tfrac{1}{3}$$

$$\underline{66}$$
$$129$$
$$\underline{99}$$
$$300$$
$$\underline{297}$$
$$3$$

⚹ Division from a Developmental Perspective

One of the first contexts in which children encounter division is in sharing—that is, the process of dividing a number of cookies, for example, among a number of people. For instance, if a young child has 7 cookies and wants to share them among 3 people, she may simply pass out the cookies—one by one—to each of the three people and have one left over (i.e., a remainder). She might or might not divide this last cookie into rough thirds. Nonetheless, little use of this experience seems to made in schools, and a child's first formal introduction to division, often around the third grade, is as an *undoing* of multiplication. For instance,

$$4 \times ? = 8$$

This is followed in the curriculum by some discussion of factors and divisors, and it culminates in the standard division algorithm.

Teachers often scaffold this process over time. Let's look at an example. Say I want to learn how to divide 1789 by 16. First I become comfortable with working with those copies of 16 that are most natural to working in a base-10 system (see Figure 6.2).

	10	6
100	1000	600
10	100	60
1	10	6

FIGURE 6.2   *Abbreviated Model: Building up Copies of 16*

The next step is to incorporate this familiarity into a somewhat efficient algorithm—an algorithm within which I choose my copies of 10 thoughtfully and, in a sense, supply a running commentary on the division process (see Figure 6.3).

```
16 )1987
      160  | 10
     1827
      800  | 50
     1027
      800  | 50

      227
      160  | 10
       67
       64  | 4
        3  └──
           124
```

FIGURE 6.3 *Early Accessible Algorithm: Taking Away Copies of 16 Until No More Remain*

In yet a later version of the division algorithm, I begin maximizing my copies of 16 to minimize the steps in the algorithm (see Figure 6.4).

```
16 )1987
     1600  | 100
      387
      320  | 20
       67
       64  | 4
        3  └──
           124
```

FIGURE 6.4   *Later Version with Fewer Steps*

P R O B L E M   6 . 3

Use the above algorithm to divide 2763 by 15.

This later version is still used in parts of the world. In U.S. schools, however, we streamline the algorithm by writing the quotient above the dividend and, by placement of digits, eliminate the trailing zeros in the subtrahends.

```
        124
16 )1987
     16
     38
     32
     67
     64
      3
```

Note that unless the scaffolding is done appropriately, the final form of the algorithm has two aspects[4] that create difficulties for children. First, it requires them to determine exactly the maximum copies of the divisor that they can take from the dividend. This feature is a source of anxiety, because students often have trouble estimating exactly how many it will take and commonly multiply trial products off to the side until they find the exact one. Second, the final form of the algorithm gives little sense of the size of the products the students are computing. In fact, they are always, as in the standard multiplication algorithm, multiplying by single digits.

✕ Whole-Number Division Algorithms

If I were to describe how I would use the standard division algorithm to divide 1987 by 16, I might proceed as follows: I examine the digits of the dividend from left to right. I can see that 16 does not divide the 1 in 1987 (actually this is 1000 and 16 *does* divide 1000; the language we use while applying the algorithm is not entirely helpful), so I check whether it divides the 19 in 1987 (actually 1900). Indeed it does with a quotient 1 (actually 100). I write the quotient above the 9 in the dividend (note that 9 is in the hundreds place) and compute the remainder (1 or, more properly, 100):

$$19 = 1 \cdot 16 + 3 \qquad \text{(actually } 1900 = 100 \cdot 16 + 300\text{)}$$

I then bring down what remains of the dividend, which gives me 387, and again, examining the digits from left to right, determine that

$$38 = 2 \cdot 16 + 6 \qquad \text{(actually } 180 = 20 \cdot 16 + 60\text{)}$$

I write the quotient 2 (actually 20) above the 8 in the dividend (note that 8 is in the tens place) and, as indicated, bring down the remainder for a result of 67. Again looking for a trial multiplier, I see that

$$67 = 4 \cdot 16 + 3$$

Writing the quotient 4 above the 7 in the dividend (note that 7 is in the units place), I have $1987 = 124 \cdot 16 + 3$. Note that placement of the digits of the quotient is critical, because this is the only record one has of their place value.

Why does it work? The formulation of division I will use is essentially that found in Euclid. It goes as follows: Let $d \neq 0$ be an arbitrary positive integer (this notion can easily be extended to negative integers). Every other integer n will either be a multiple of d or fall between two consecutive multiples of d— that is, between $q \cdot d$ and $(q + 1)d$. Thus one can write[5]

$$n = q \cdot d + r$$

---

[4] K. C. Fuson, Developing mathematical power in whole number operations. In *A Research Companion to NCTM's Standards*, ed. J. Kilpatrick, W. G. Martin, and D. Schifter (Reston, VA: NCTM, 2003).
[5] That this can be uniquely done is assumed without proof.

where r is one of the numbers

$$0, 1, 2, \ldots, d - 1$$

The job in division is, given a dividend n and a divisor d, to determine the quotient q and the remainder r. In my example above, that means finding q and r such that

$$1987 = q \cdot 16 + r$$

where r is a positive integer and $0 \leq r < 16$ (that is, r is one of the numbers $0, 1, 2, \ldots, 15$).

In base-10 this becomes a problem of finding r and

$$q = q_m 10^m + q_{m-1} 10^{m-1} + \cdots + q_1 10^1 + q_0$$

such that

$$
\begin{aligned}
n &= (q_m 10^m + q_{m-1} 10^{m-1} + \cdots + q_1 10^1 + q_0) \cdot 16 + r \\
&= q_m 10^m \cdot 16 + q_{m-1} 10^{m-1} \cdot 16 + \cdots + q_1 10^1 \cdot 16 + q_0 \cdot 16 + r
\end{aligned}
$$

and $0 \leq r < 16$.

We can rewrite n as

$$n = Q_m \cdot (10^m \cdot 16) + R_m$$

where

$$Q_m = q_m$$

and

$$R_m = q_{m-1} 10^{m-1} \cdot 16 + \cdots + q_1 10^1 \cdot 16 + q_0 \cdot 16 + r$$

Note that $0 \leq q_{m-1} 10^{m-1} + \cdots + q_1 10^1 + q_0 < 10^m$ so that $0 \leq R_m < 10^m \cdot 16$. A similar argument shows that the problem

$$R_m = Q_{m-1} \cdot (10^{m-1} \cdot 16) + R_{m-1}$$

has the solution

$$
\begin{aligned}
Q_{m-1} &= q_{m-1} \\
R_{m-1} &= q_{m-2} 10^{m-2} \cdot 16 + \cdots + q_1 10^1 \cdot 16 + q_0 \cdot 16 + r
\end{aligned}
$$

where $0 \leq R_{m-1} < 10^m \cdot 16$. Because we can continue this, you can see that, in base 10, I need only solve a series of division problems involving, in effect, single-digit quotients.

Let me demonstrate how all this goes and its correspondence to the standard division algorithm with my example.[6] As usual, I write the dividend 1987 in expanded notation:

$$1 \cdot 10^3 + 9 \cdot 10^2 + 8 \cdot 10^1 + 7 \cdot 1$$

---

[6] The underlined parts of my illustration on page 89 are those that correspond to steps in the standard addition algorithm.

The largest copy of 16 that could possibly work is $16 \cdot 10^3$. However,

$$1 \cdot 10^3 + 9 \cdot 10^2 + 8 \cdot 10^1 + 7 \cdot 1 = 0 \cdot (16 \cdot 10^3) + 1 \cdot 10^3 + 9 \cdot 10^2 + 8 \cdot 10^1 + 7 \cdot 1$$

How about $16 \cdot 10^2$? Well,

$$1 \cdot 10^3 + 9 \cdot 10^2 + 8 \cdot 10^1 + 7 \cdot 1 = 1 \cdot (16 \cdot 10^2) + \underline{387}$$

and

$$387 = 2 \cdot (16 \cdot 10^1) + \underline{67}$$

Finally,

$$67 = 4 \cdot (16) + \underline{3}$$

so

$$1987 = 124 \cdot 16 + 3$$

Let me try this with base-8 to give a better view of the structure of the algorithm. I may need a multiplication table, such as that shown in Figure 6.5.

x	1	2	3	4	5	6	7
1	1	2	3	4	5	6	7
2	2	4	6	10	12	14	16
3	3	6	11	14	17	22	25
4	4	10	14	20	24	30	34
5	5	12	17	24	31	36	43
6	6	14	22	30	36	44	52
7	7	16	25	34	43	52	61

FIGURE 6.5   *Base-8 Multiplication Table*

How about 1567_8 divided by 14_8? Well,

$$
\begin{array}{r}
111_8 \\
14_8 \overline{)1567_8} \\
14_8 \\
\hline
16_8 \\
14_8 \\
\hline
27_8 \\
14_8 \\
\hline
13_8
\end{array}
$$

Simple, isn't it?

P R O B L E M   6 . 4

Divide 2763_8 by 15_8.

⚹ Clock and Modular Arithmetic

Up to this point, I have been writing about the integers and usual applications of the arithmetic operations. However, there are situations where these usual applications are not applicable. Have you considered, for example, how minutes add on a clock? (Seconds with respect to minutes, hours with respect to days, and days with respect to years behave in a similar manner.) Instead of adding on a number line,

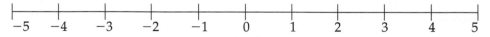

one adds on a circle.

Thus, focusing on the minute hand, we have

$$1 \text{ hour } 59 \text{ minutes}$$

$$+ \underline{\hspace{1.5em} 2 \text{ minutes}}$$

$$2 \text{ hours } 1 \text{ minute}$$

Subtraction is equally bothersome:

$$2 \text{ hours } 1 \text{ minute}$$

$$- \underline{\hspace{1.5em} 2 \text{ minutes}}$$

$$1 \text{ hour } 59 \text{ minutes}$$

And so, twirling that minute hand, is multiplication:

$$5 \cdot 54 \text{ minutes} = 270 \text{ minutes}$$

$$= 6 \text{ hours } 30 \text{ minutes}$$

All this seems very different from, and much more complicated than, ordinary arithmetic in a base-10 system.

Nonetheless, Karl Friedrich Gauss, in the mid-eighteenth century, showed with the notion of congruence that clock arithmetic is much more obvious and quite a bit more intriguing than it might seem at first glance. Gauss introduces his congruences through the following definition:[7]

> Two integers a and b are be said to be congruent for the modulus m when their difference $a - b$ is divisible by the integer m.

---

[7] Oystein Ore, *Number Theory and Its History* (New York: McGraw-Hill, 1948), p. 212.

This he expresses in the symbolic statement

$$a \equiv b \,(\text{mod } m)$$

When a and b are not congruent, they are called incongruent for the modulus m, and this is written

$$a \not\equiv b \,(\text{mod } m)$$

Let me illustrate the definitions with a few examples. We know, for instance, that

$$26 \equiv 16 \,(\text{mod } 5)$$

because the difference $26 - 16 = 10$ is divisible by 5. Also,

$$59 \equiv -1 \,(\text{mod } 60)$$

because $59 - (-1) = 60$ is divisible by 60, whereas

$$3 \not\equiv 11 \,(\text{mod } 7)$$

because $3 - 11 = -8$ is *not* divisible by 7.

An alternative definition of congruence that will be useful is that b is congruent to a when it differs from a by a multiple of m:

$$b = a + k \cdot m$$

In our examples above,

$$26 = 16 + 2 \cdot 5$$

and

$$59 = (-1) + 1 \cdot 60$$

Finally, I note that if

$$n = q \cdot d + r$$

then

$$n \equiv r \,(\text{mod } d)$$

For instance,

$$26 = 4 \cdot 5 + 6$$

and, allowing negative remainders,

$$59 = 1 \cdot 60 + (-1)$$

Thus, the arithmetic of congruences is the arithmetic of remainders.

Let's take a closer look at some of the particulars of that arithmetic. Here are some basic properties of the congruence that we will find useful.

1. **Reflexivity.**   I have

$$a \equiv a \,(\text{mod } m)$$

for any modulus m.

Proof: I note that $a - a = 0$ is a multiple of any number m (that is, $m \cdot 0 = 0$).

2. **Symmetry.** When

$$a \equiv b \,(\text{mod } m)$$

then I also have

$$b \equiv a \,(\text{mod } m)$$

Proof: The difference $a - b$ is just the difference $b - a$ with the sign reversed. So if $a - b$ is divisible by m, so is $b - a$.

3. **Transitivity.** When

$$a \equiv b \,(\text{mod } m) \quad \text{and} \quad b \equiv c \,(\text{mod } m)$$

then

$$a \equiv c \,(\text{mod } m)$$

Proof: To prove this, I need only observe that

$$a - c = (a - b) + (b - c)$$

is divisible by m since $a - b$ and $b - c$ are divisible by m.

4. **Additivity.** If

$$a \equiv b \,(\text{mod } m)$$
$$c \equiv d \,(\text{mod } m)$$

then

$$(a + c) \equiv (b + d) \,(\text{mod } m) \qquad\qquad \text{(B)}$$

and

$$(a - c) \equiv (b - d) \,(\text{mod } m) \qquad\qquad \text{(C)}$$

Proof: I need only observe that

$$(a + c) - (b + d) = (a - b) + (c - d)$$
$$(a - c) - (b - d) = (a - b) - (c - d)$$

and $(a + c) - (b + d)$ and $(a - c) - (b - d)$ are divisible by m, because $a - b$ and $c - d$ are divisible by m.

5. **Multiplicativity.** For any integer k, if

$$a \equiv b \,(\text{mod } m)$$

then

$$k \cdot a \equiv k \cdot b \,(\text{mod } m)$$

Proof: I need only observe that

$$k \cdot a - k \cdot b = k(a - b)$$

Hence $k \cdot a - k \cdot b$ is divisible by m because a is congruent to b.

Let's see how all this works on the clock. I'll focus on the minute hand. By reflexivity,

$$2 \equiv 2 \ (\text{mod } 60)$$
$$59 \equiv 59 \ (\text{mod } 60)$$

so their sum (using additivity) would be

$$61 \equiv 61 \ (\text{mod } 60) \quad (\text{using additivity})$$

However,

$$61 \equiv 1 \ (\text{mod } 60) \quad (\text{That is, } 61 - 1 - 1 \cdot 60.)$$

so by transitivity,

$$2 + 59 \equiv 1 \ (\text{mod } 60)$$

In like manner,

$$1 \equiv 1 \ (\text{mod } 60)$$
$$2 \equiv 2 \ (\text{mod } 60)$$

so their difference would be

$$-1 \equiv -1 \ (\text{mod } 60)$$

However,

$$-1 \equiv 59 \ (\text{mod } 60) \quad (\text{That is, } -1 - 59 = -1 \cdot 60.)$$

so by transitivity,

$$1 - 2 \equiv 59 \ (\text{mod } 60)$$

So far, so good. How about multiplication? Well,

$$5 \cdot 54 \equiv 270 \ (\text{mod } 60)$$

so

$$270 \equiv 30 \ (\text{mod } 60) \quad (\text{That is, } 270 - 30 = 4 \cdot 60.)$$

This is correct, but let me do it another way:

$$54 \equiv -6 \ (\text{mod } 60) \quad (\text{That is, } 54 - (-6) = 1 \cdot 60.)$$

so by multiplicativity,

$$5 \cdot 54 \equiv -5 \cdot -6 \ (\text{mod } 60)$$
$$\equiv -30 \ (\text{mod } 60)$$

Now

$$-30 \equiv 30 \ (\text{mod } 60) \quad (\text{That is, } -30 - 30 = -1 \cdot 60.)$$

so by transitivity,

$$5 \cdot 54 \equiv 30 \ (\text{mod } 60)$$

All this, I suggest, seems to save a considerable amount of multiplication and division and deserves to be explored further.

P R O B L E M   6 . 5

Give the smallest non-negative solution to each of the following, and explain your reasoning.

   a. $245 \equiv ?$ (mod 60)
   b. $250 \equiv ?$ (mod 60)
   c. $490 \equiv ?$ (mod 60)

✖ Divisibility Rules

A staple of the upper elementary and middle school grades is the topic of divisibility. For example, we might ask students whether 156793452 is divisible by 2, and many of them would tell us that if a number ends in 0, 2, 4, or 8, this is indeed the case. Another interesting mathematical question is whether such a number is divisible by 3. This seems harder, although it turns out that if the sum of the digits is divisible by 3, then so is the number. One nice feature of congruence is that it makes this reasonably obvious.

Let me show this by beginning with a smaller number such as 2241. In expanded notation, this is

$$2 \cdot 10^3 + 2 \cdot 10^2 + 4 \cdot 10^1 + 1 \cdot 1$$

I know that

$$10 \equiv 1 \ (\text{mod } 3) \quad (\text{That is, } 10 - 1 = 3 \cdot 3.)$$

and thus, by multiplicativity,

$$10^n \equiv 1 \ (\text{mod } 3)$$

for any $n > 0$. I also know that

$$4 \cdot 10^n \equiv 4 \cdot 1 \ (\text{mod } 3) \quad (\text{by multiplicativity})$$

In fact, I know that for any integer a,

$$a \cdot 10^n \equiv a \cdot 1 \ (\text{mod } 3)$$

P R O B L E M   6 . 6

Prove that for any integer a,

$$a \cdot 10^n \equiv a \cdot 1 \ (\text{mod } 3)$$

Using these facts and considering 2241 place by place, I have

$$2 \cdot 10^3 + 2 \cdot 10^2 + 4 \cdot 10^1 + 1 \cdot 1 \equiv 2 \cdot 1 + 2 \cdot 1 + 4 \cdot 1 + 1 \cdot 1 \ (\mathrm{mod}\ 3)$$
$$\equiv 9 \ (\mathrm{mod}\ 3)$$
$$= 0 \ (\mathrm{mod}\ 3)$$

and hence 2241 is divisible by 3. Applying this to 156793452 gives

$$156793452 = 1 + 5 + 6 + 7 + 9 + 3 + 4 + 5 + 2 \ (\mathrm{mod}\ 3)$$
$$\equiv 1 + 5 + 6 \ (\mathrm{mod}\ 3)$$
$$\equiv 12 \ (\mathrm{mod}\ 3)$$
$$\equiv 0 \ \mathrm{mod}\ 3$$

Thus 156793452 is divisible by 3.

P R O B L E M   6 . 7

(a) What is the divisibility rule for 9? Explain your thinking. (b) What is the divisibility rule for 11? Explain your thinking.

⚹ Casting Out Nines

Imagine that you have worked on a moderately long multiplication problem—for example, 4321×726—and obtained an answer of 3127046. You could, of course, check by dividing 3127046 by 726 to see whether you obtained a quotient of 4321. However, you could also check by *casting out nines* as follows:

4321:	$4 + 3 + 2 + 1 = 10$	and	$10 - 9 = 1$
726:	$7 + 2 + 6 = 15$	and	$15 - 9 = 6$
3127046:	$3 + 1 + 2 + 7 + 0 + 4 + 6 = 23$	and	$23 - 9 - 9 = 5$

The fact that $1 \times 6 \neq 5$ means you have multiplied incorrectly. The correct product is 3137046. Note that

3137046: $3 + 1 + 3 + 7 + 0 + 4 + 6 = 24$ and $24 - 9 - 9 = \underline{6}$

The technique of casting out nines or *check of nines* is found in the works of various Arab writers—for instance, al-Khowârizmî (c. AD 825)—and was employed for checking all varieties of arithmetical operations. This check was employed in U.S. arithmetics in the 1700s but dropped out of U.S. arithmetics during the eighteenth century and reappeared in the 1900s.

How does it work? The technique is fairly straightforward. As you should have shown in the previous section,

$$4321 \equiv 4 + 3 + 2 + 1 \ (\mathrm{mod}\ 9)$$
$$\equiv 1 \ (\mathrm{mod}\ 9)$$
$$726 = 7 + 2 + 6 \ (\mathrm{mod}\ 9)$$
$$\equiv 6 \ (\mathrm{mod}\ 9)$$

Now, by multiplicativity,

$$726 \cdot 4321 \equiv 6 \cdot 4321 \pmod 9$$
$$6 \cdot 4321 \equiv 6 \cdot 1 \pmod 9$$

so by transitivity,

$$726 \cdot 4321 \equiv 6 \cdot 1 \pmod 9$$

On the other hand,

$$\begin{aligned} 3137046 &\equiv 3 + 1 + 3 + 7 + 0 + 4 + 6 \pmod 9 \\ &\equiv 6 \pmod 9 \end{aligned}$$

PROBLEM 6.8

Use *casting out nines* to check your addition of 2345789 + 9987234.

Note that this check can fail, although it seems fairly reliable for *small* errors. That is, you may have done the computation incorrectly and the check may fail to catch your error. For example, 28 + 28 ≠ 65; however, *casting out nines* will show no error. On the other hand, suppose we also cast out elevens. Then

$$28 = 2 \cdot 11 + \underline{6} \quad \text{and} \quad 65 = 5 \cdot 11 + \underline{10}\ (\text{or } 6 \cdot 11 + (-1))$$

or, using the rules you devised for divisibility by 11,

$$\begin{aligned} 28 &\equiv -2 + 8 \pmod{11} \quad \text{and} \quad & 65 &\equiv -6 + 5 \pmod{11} \\ &\equiv 6 \pmod{11} & &\equiv -1 \pmod{11} \end{aligned}$$

Thus, casting out nines together with casting out elevens seems a little more reliable.

PROBLEM 6.9

Use *casting out elevens* to check your addition of 2345789 + 9987234.

Indeterminate Problems Yet Again

Congruences provide the ideal tools for solving linear indeterminate problems. Let's return to the plantain problem of Chapter 3:

> Into the bright and refreshing outskirts of a forest, which were full of numerous trees, with the branches bent down with the weight of flowers and fruits, trees, such as jambu trees, date-palms, hintala trees, palymyras, punnaga trees, and mango trees—filled with many sounds of crowds of

parrots and cuckoos found near springs containing lotuses with bees roaming around them—a number of travelers entered with joy.

There are 63 equal heaps of plantain fruits put together and 7 single fruits. These were divided evenly among 23 travelers. Tell me the number of fruits in each heap.

As I noted there, if I let F be the number of plantain fruits in each heap and let T be the fruits allocated to each traveler, then I have the equation

$$63 \cdot F + 7 = 23 \cdot T \tag{D}$$

Okay, let's use congruences. Well,

$$63 \cdot F + 7 \equiv 23 \cdot T \pmod{7}$$

or

$$23 \cdot T \equiv 0 \pmod{7}$$

so $2 \cdot T \equiv 0 \pmod{7}$, and thus, for some integer R, $2 \cdot T = 7 \cdot R$. Now

$$2 \cdot T \equiv 7 \cdot R \pmod{2} \rightarrow R \equiv 0 \pmod{2}$$

so for some integer S, $R = 2 \cdot S$, and hence, $T = 7 \cdot S$. Substituting this in (D) and doing a little algebra, we find

$$9 \cdot F + 1 = 23 \cdot S \tag{E}$$

Now

$$9 \cdot F + 1 \equiv 23 \cdot S \pmod{9}$$

and so

$$1 \equiv 23 \cdot S \pmod{9} \rightarrow 5 \cdot S \equiv 1 \pmod{9}$$

Thus for some integer U, $5 \cdot S = 1 + 9 \cdot U$, and

$$5 \cdot S \equiv 1 + 9 \cdot U \pmod{5} \rightarrow 4 \cdot U + 1 \equiv 0 \pmod{5}$$

Thus for some integer V, $4 \cdot U + 1 = 5 \cdot V$, and hence,

$$4 \cdot U + 1 \equiv 5 \cdot V \pmod{4} \rightarrow V \equiv 1 \pmod{4}$$

So there is some integer Q such that

$$V = 1 + 4 \cdot Q \tag{F}$$

Okay, substituting (F) in the expression for U,

$$4 \cdot U + 1 = 5 \cdot V$$

and substituting that in the expression for S,

$$5 \cdot S = 1 + 9 \cdot U$$

and substituting that in expression (E) gives

$$U = 1 + 5 \cdot Q$$
$$S = 2 + 9 \cdot Q$$

and

$$T = 14 + 63 \cdot Q$$
$$F = 5 + 23 \cdot Q$$

P R O B L E M   6 . 1 0

Solve the following problem using congruences: Pencils cost 15 cents and erasers cost 10 cents. If you are to spend exactly $2.00 (forget about tax) what are the different combinations of pencils and erasers you can buy?

Investigations

1. Oystein Ore recounts[8] a letter he received during World War II from a group of "bewildered" GIs at Guadalcanal. The problem they wished to solve follows.

   A man has a theatre with a seating capacity of 100. He wishes to admit 100 people in such a proportion that will enable him to take in $1.00 with prices as follows: men 5¢, women 2¢, children 10 for 1¢. How many of each can be admitted?

   Help these GIs out with your solution. [*Hint:* If you write out the conditions, you get the two simultaneous equations

   $$x + y + z = 100$$
   $$5x + 2y + \frac{z}{10} = 100$$

   where x is the number of men, y is the number of women, and z is the number of children. Eliminate one of the variables between these two equations and solve via congruences.]

2. In 1640 Pierre de Fermat claimed, in essence,[9] that for any integer N and any prime p, it is the case that

   $$N^p \equiv N \pmod{p}$$

   Leonard Euler, in 1736, was the first to publish a proof. Let's you and I do a proof. I will ask you to justify some of the steps I take.

   Well, Fermat's claim (this is termed Fermat's Little Theorem) is certainly true if $N = 0$ or p is a divisor of N. Therefore, I'll assume that neither is the case and, hence, that $0 < N < p$ [(a) Justify this step.]. In this case, I need only prove [(b) Justify this step.] that

   $$N^{p-1} \equiv 1 \pmod{p}$$

   Consider the following sequence of numbers:

   $$N, 2 \cdot N, 3 \cdot N, ..., (p-1) \cdot N \qquad\qquad\qquad (G)$$

---

[8] *Number Theory and Its History*, p. 124.
[9] I have restated his claim in congruence notation.

and reduce each one modulo p. The resulting sequence will be a rearrangement [(c) Justify this step.] of

$$1, 2, 3, \ldots, (p-1) \tag{H}$$

If I multiply the numbers together in these two sequences, I have

$$(N) \cdot (2) \cdot (3 \cdot N) \cdot \cdots \cdot ((p-1) \cdot N) \equiv 1 \cdot 2 \cdot 3 \cdot \cdots \cdot (p-1) \pmod{p} \text{ or}$$

or

$$N^{p-1}(1 \cdot 2 \cdot 3 \cdot \cdots \cdot (p-1)) \equiv 1 \cdot 2 \cdot 3 \cdot \cdots \cdot (p-1) \pmod{p}$$

Canceling [(d) Justify this step.] on both sides gives

$$N^{p-1} = 1 \pmod{p}$$

as was to be shown.

3. Use Fermat's Little Theorem to prove that for a prime p—other than 2 or 5—there is an integer of the form

$$999999\cdots 9$$

that is divisible by p. Can you generalize this result? Can you prove something similar for numbers of the following form?

$$11111\cdots 1$$

4. Casting out both nines and elevens seems to provide fairly effective arithmetic checks, especially for large-digit arithmetic operations. However, as I demonstrated for nines, such checks do not catch all errors. Create an addition error that casting out both nines and elevens fails to catch.

Fractions

Up to this point, we have taken a reasonably careful look at the art of computing with integers (we focused primarily on the positive integers but I briefly sketched the extension to the negative integers). Now it is time to introduce another species of numbers into the discussion. *Rational numbers* or, as they are commonly called, fractions,[1] arise naturally in problems of the following sort:

> Nadia wants to share 5 cookies with her friend Ysabel.
> How many will each one get?

or

$$? 3 4 = 5$$

In this chapter, you and I will explore the notion of equivalent fractions and how one adds, subtracts, multiplies, and divides fractions. We will also take a brief look at the notion of proportionality.

✄ Fractions from a Historical Perspective

Multiplication is vexation,

Division is as bad,

The Rule of Three perplexes me,

And Fractions drive me mad.[2]

Fractions have always been a source of difficulty for students of the art of arithmetic. Early Babylonian and Egyptian arithmetic called for proficiency with fractions. Rather than having any notion of numerator and denominator, Egyptians focused on unit fractions—that is, fractions with what is essentially a numerator of 1 (two-thirds was the only anomaly). This system avoided having to deal with a numerator, but it also required the writing of long series of fractions to

---

[1] Note that fractions include the integers and mixed numbers.
[2] Louis Charles Karpinski, *The History of Arithmetic* (Chicago: Rand McNally, 1925), pp. 121–129.

express quantities such as seven-eighths. For instance, seven-eighths was written as $\frac{1}{2}, \frac{1}{4}, \frac{1}{8}$ or as $\frac{2}{3}, \frac{1}{8}, \frac{1}{12}$. That is,

$$\frac{7}{8} = \frac{1}{2} + \frac{1}{4} + \frac{1}{8}$$

and

$$\frac{7}{8} = \frac{2}{3} + \frac{1}{8} + \frac{1}{12}$$

P R O B L E M   7 . 1

(a) Write $\frac{3}{5}$ in unit fractions; (b) write $\frac{7}{18}$ in unit fractions.

The Babylonians used sexagesimal fractions—that is, fractions with denominators of 60 and powers of 60—a representation that has similarities to our present decimal notation. In addition, Babylonian astronomy greatly influenced Greek astronomy. This influence is still present in astronomical calculations. For instance, the terms *minutes* and *seconds* come from the Latin *minutiae primae, minutiae secundae*, meaning "first fractions," "second fractions," and so on.

The Romans followed the Babylonian pattern. The base chosen was 12. Special symbols and names were devised and used for $\frac{1}{12}$ to $\frac{11}{12}$, for $\frac{1}{8}$ as well as one and one-half twelfths, for $\frac{1}{24}, \frac{1}{36}, \frac{1}{48}, \frac{1}{96}, \frac{1}{144}$, and on to even smaller fractions. For example,

duella	$\dfrac{1}{36}$
tremissis	$\dfrac{1}{216}$
chalcus	$\dfrac{1}{2304}$

These names and symbols were used from approximately the tenth until the thirteenth century.[3]

Egyptian fractions, including $\frac{2}{3}$, were extensively used in Greek arithmetic. As discussed in the previous chapter, the Ahmes papyrus contains the problem 19 divided by 8. As we saw, the results were expressed in unit fractions. The Greek papyri, many centuries later, include the same problems couched in somewhat more abstract terms. The Greeks employed common fractions as well as sexagesimal fractions.

The fractional notation used in India was similar to that of today, although it omitted the bar. Thus $\frac{3}{11}$ would be written

$$3$$
$$11$$

---

[3] See, for example, Karpinski, p. 125.

and $8\frac{3}{11}$ was written

$$8$$
$$3$$
$$11$$

Brahmagupta and other Indian scholars gave extensive instructions for the fundamental operations with fractions. Bháskara, as a case in point, writes: "After reversing the numerator and denominator of the divisor, the remaining process for division of fractions is that of multiplication."[4]

The modern treatment of common fractions and the terminology for them appear in Recorde's *The Grounde of Artes*. However, the term *common fraction* or *vulgar fraction* was coined after the introduction of decimal fractions in order to distinguish ordinary fractions and sexagesimal fractions from decimal fractions.

✂ Fractions from a Developmental Perspective

In the primary grades, students use a variety of strategies to solve fair-sharing problems. For instance, when trying to share three cookies between two children, another child may divide each of the cookies into two equal pieces (halves) and give each child a half of each cookie $\left(\frac{1}{2} + \frac{1}{2} + \frac{1}{2} = \frac{3}{2}\right)$, or one cookie and a half of the other $\left(1\frac{1}{2}\right)$. To understand the process and the equivalence of the two strategies, a child must, at least informally, recognize that

> The shares must be "fair," or equal in size.
> Three halves literally means three one-halves.
> Three halves and one and a half represent the same amount.

Fraction addition is not much of a concern in the primary grades. Nonetheless, a number of children understand that two halves $\left(\frac{1}{2} + \frac{1}{2}\right)$ make a whole.

P R O B L E M   7 . 2

You have 3 dozen donuts to divide fairly among 5 people. What fraction of a dozen does each person get?

By the beginning of the upper elementary grades, students build on such experiences with fractions and on further instruction to construct a part-whole conception of fractions. That is, they begin to conceive of a fraction as a whole composed of a specific number of distinct parts:

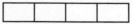

---

[4] Karpinski, p. 126.

However, students think of fractions in terms of parts making up the whole rather than as single quantities resulting from the partitioning of a unit. For instance, students frequently refer to the fraction $\frac{3}{4}$ as "three pieces of a pizza or cake that is cut into four pieces" or say," You have three pieces of pizza and there's four in all."[5] Hence, students' informal strategies for fraction problems often treat fraction problems as whole-number-partitioning problems. The following dialogue[6] illustrates such thinking.

Ms. Toich: Suppose you have two lemon pies and you eat $\frac{1}{5}$ of one pie. How much lemon pie do you have left?

Ned: You'd have $1\frac{4}{5}$. First of all, you had $\frac{5}{5}$ to start with. Then if you ate one you'd have four pieces left out of the five, and you would still have one whole pie left.

As children move further into upper elementary grades, they progress from treating fractions as whole-number-partitioning problems to recognizing them as a form of portioning that takes into account the size of individual fractions. You might say that this development takes place on the number line. The following dialogue[7] is illustrative.

Ms. Toich: Pretend that you have $\frac{4}{5}$ of a chocolate cake and I give you $\frac{9}{10}$ more. How much chocolate cake do you have?

Bob: (wrote $\frac{4}{5} + \frac{9}{10} = 1\frac{2}{3}$) About $1\frac{2}{3}$, because $\frac{4}{5}$ is $\frac{1}{5}$ away from a whole and $\frac{9}{10}$ is $\frac{1}{10}$ away from a whole, so they're both about a whole, but then they're also one away, $\frac{1}{5}$ and $\frac{1}{10}$ away from a whole, so I thought of $\frac{2}{3}$, 'cause a fifth and a tenth are about $\frac{2}{3}$, I mean $\frac{1}{3}$.

PROBLEM 7.3

Jim is given $\frac{14}{15}$ of a pie. Mary is given $\frac{13}{14}$ of a pie of the same size. "That's not fair," Jim says, "Mary's got more pie than I since her pieces are bigger!" Mary replies, "That's not true. Jim's got more pie than I since he has more pieces!" Who has more pie, Mary or Jim, and why?

Decimals are introduced in the final years of elementary school, and children eagerly accept the possibility of replacing, for instance, $\frac{1}{2}$ by 0.5 and returning to the algorithms of youth.

Fraction Arithmetic

As I have noted, most discussions of fractions in the primary grades is grounded in the notion of the whole (or one might say the unit) and associated partitioning problems. However, I'm going to situate my discussion of fraction arithmetic on

[5] Nancy Mack, Confounding whole-number concepts and fraction concepts when building on informal knowledge, *Journal for Research in Mathematics Education*, 26 (1995).
[6] Adapted from Mack, p. 434.
[7] Adapted from Mack, p. 436.

the number line and conceive of a fraction as a sort of magnitude. In particular (much as I did for negative integers and for quite similar reasons), I will begin by defining a fraction as the solution x to an equation of the form[8]

$$b \cdot x = a \qquad \boxed{5 \cdot x = 2} \qquad \text{(A)}$$

where a and b are integers and $b \neq 0$. Here b is the number of parts in the whole, and a is the number of those parts that I am selecting. The fraction x is that piece—that is, a out of b parts—that I break off from the whole. That is, if I have broken the whole into 5 pieces and selected 2 of those pieces, then I have broken off $\frac{2}{5}$ of the whole.

Such a definition will enable me to develop algorithms for fractions that (like those developed for the negative integers) follow naturally from the structure of the mathematics. When $a = 1$, I have

$$b \cdot x = 1 \qquad \boxed{5 \cdot x = 1} \qquad \text{(A)}$$

That is, x is the unit fraction $\frac{1}{b}$ and, hence, one of the b equal subdivisions of unity. For example, 1 of the 5 equal parts of this unit rectangle is represented by the unit fraction $\frac{1}{5}$:

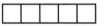

Equivalent Fractions

The quantity $\frac{1}{2}$ is the solution of the equation

$$2 \cdot x = 1 \qquad \boxed{2 \cdot \frac{1}{2} = 1}$$

However, it is also the solution of the equation

$$4 \cdot x = 2 \qquad \boxed{4 \cdot \frac{1}{2} = 2}$$

In fact, if k is a non-zero integer, then $\frac{1}{2}$ is the solution to any equation of the form

$$2k \cdot x = k \qquad \boxed{2 \cdot 4 \cdot \frac{1}{2} = 4}$$

---

[8] In outlined boxes on the right, illustrative examples are provided.

just as are all fractions of the form $\frac{k}{2k}$. We say (and this may be a remnant of the part-whole conception of fraction) that $\frac{1}{2}$ is equivalent to $\frac{k}{2k}$ on the number line, of course,

$$\frac{1}{2} = \frac{k}{2k}$$

$$\frac{1}{2} = \frac{4}{2 \cdot 4}$$

A portion of the elementary mathematics curriculum focuses on determining when two fractions are equivalent and on representing a fraction in a more useful equivalent form (essentially what is termed *reduction*). The first of these tasks is straightforward. Say we have fractions

x and y (that is, $\frac{a}{b}, \frac{c}{d}$)

x and y (that is, $\frac{2}{3}, \frac{8}{12}$)

satisfying equations

$$b \cdot x = a$$
$$d \cdot y = c$$

$$3 \cdot x = 2$$
$$12 \cdot y = 8$$

respectively. We wish to determine when $x = y$, or $x - y = 0$. Multiplying the first of these equations by d and the second by b, we have

$$d \cdot b \cdot x = d \cdot a$$
$$b \cdot d \cdot y = b \cdot c$$

$$12 \cdot 3 \cdot x = 12 \cdot 2$$
$$3 \cdot 12 \cdot y = 3 \cdot 8$$

Subtracting yields

$$d \cdot b \cdot x - b \cdot d \cdot y = d \cdot a - b \cdot c$$

$$12 \cdot 3 \cdot x - 3 \cdot 12 \cdot y$$
$$= 12 \cdot 2 - 3 \cdot 8$$ (B)

or

$$d \cdot b\,(x - y) = d \cdot a - b \cdot c$$

$$12 \cdot 3 \cdot (x - y) = 12 \cdot 2\,2\,3 \cdot 8$$

so

$$x = y \quad \text{(that is, } \frac{a}{b} = \frac{c}{d}\text{)}$$

$$x = y \quad \text{(that is, } \frac{2}{3} = \frac{8}{12}\text{)}$$

if and only if

$$d \cdot a = b \cdot c$$

$$12 \cdot 2 = 3 \cdot 8$$ (C)

Note that $x > y$ (that is, $\frac{a}{b} > \frac{c}{d}$) is equivalent to $x - y > 0$. This is equivalent to

$$d \cdot b\,(x - y) > 0$$

and hence, according to (B), is equivalent to

$$d \cdot a - b \cdot c > 0$$

or

$$d \cdot a > b \cdot c \qquad \text{(D)}$$

For example, $\frac{1}{2} > \frac{2}{5}$ since

$$5 \cdot 1 > 2 \cdot 2$$

The second of these tasks, *reduction,* is a bit more complicated. What we need to do, given a fraction $\frac{a}{b}$, is to find a *minimal* equivalent. This, I suggest, is the same as finding the largest positive integer k such that k divides a and k divides b. Such a k, by the way, is called the greatest common divisor of a and b. Although we can guess the value of k, it can also be systematically determined.[9] For this, a procedure called Euclid's algorithm (which occurs in the seventh book of his *Elements*) is quite useful.

> *Euclid's algorithm:* I'll assume, without loss of generality, that $b \geq a$. I divide b by a with respect to the least positive remainder.

$$b = q_1 \cdot a + r_1 \qquad 0 \leq r_1 < a$$

$$\begin{array}{ccc} b & a & r_1 \\ 63 = 1 \cdot 33 & + & 30 \end{array}$$

If r_1 is not zero (in which case the algorithm terminates), then[10] I divide a by r_1

$$a = q_1 \cdot r_1 + r_2 \qquad 0 \leq r_2 < r_1$$

$$\begin{array}{ccc} a & r_1 & r_2 \\ 33 = 1 \cdot 30 & + & 3 \end{array}$$

and continue this process on r_1 and r_2, and so on. Since the remainders $r_1, r_2, \ldots$ form a decreasing sequence of positive integers, one must eventually arrive at a division for which $r_{n+1} = 0$.

$$b = q_1 \cdot a + r_1$$
$$a = q_2 \cdot r_1 + r_2$$
$$r_1 = q_3 \cdot r_2 + r_3$$
$$\vdots$$
$$r_{n-2} = q_n \cdot r_{n-1} + r_n$$
$$r_{n-1} = q_{n+1} \cdot r_n + 0$$

$$63 = 1 \cdot 33 + 30$$
$$33 = 1 \cdot 30 + 3$$

$$30 = 10 \cdot 3 + 0$$

Now r_n is a common divisor of a and b. We can see this from my last step that r_n divides r_{n-1}. The next to the last division shows that r_n divides r_{n-2} because it divides both terms on the right, and so on. Thus r_n must divide

---

[9] Which is nice if, though I suspect it is quite unlikely, you are asked to quickly reduce the fraction $\frac{63,020}{76,084}$.
[10] Note how the previous divisor and remainder become the subsequent dividend and divisor, respectively.

a and b. On the other hand, every divisor of a and b must divide r_n. To see this, let c be a divisor of a and b. Then, in the first step, c divides r_1 and, in the second, c divides r_2. Continuing the process, we see that c divides r_n. Thus every divisor of a and b divides r_n, and hence r_n is the greatest common divisor of a and b.

Let's consider an example. Say I want to reduce the fraction $\frac{63,020}{76,084}$ to its lowest terms. I have

$$76,084 = 63,020 \cdot 1 + 13,064$$
$$63,020 = 13,064 \cdot 4 + 10764$$
$$13,064 = 10,764 \cdot 1 + 2300$$
$$10,764 = 2,300 \cdot 4 + 1564$$
$$2,300 = 1,564 \cdot 1 + 736$$
$$1,564 = 736 \cdot 2 + 92$$
$$736 = 92 \cdot 8$$

Thus the greatest common divisor is 92, and hence

$$\frac{63,020}{76,084} = \frac{92 \cdot 685}{92 \cdot 827}$$

$$= \frac{685}{827}$$

P R O B L E M   7 . 4

How do we know that this is the *least* reduction? Assume that it isn't, and show that this assumption leads to a contradiction.

P R O B L E M   7 . 5

What is the greatest common divisor of (a) 2754 and 34; (b) 101 and 435?

Fraction Addition and Subtraction Algorithms

Fraction addition, on the surface, seems quite different from addition of whole numbers. This is partly because we insist on expressing a sum of fractions as a single number (in this we differ, for example, from the Egyptians, where a sum of unit fractions was allowed) and partly because of a possible variation in the whole (or, effectively, denominator) among fractions in the sum. This latter difference does, however, appear in whole-number arithmetic when we consider the analogous idea of units. As a case in point, if I were to add

$$5 \text{ yards} + 4 \text{ feet}$$

I would need either to convert both 5 yards and 4 feet to inches or to convert the 5 yards to feet. That is,

$$5 \cdot 36 \text{ inches} + 4 \cdot 12 \text{ inches} = 228 \text{ inches}$$

or

$$5 \cdot 3 \text{ feet} + 4 \text{ feet} = 19 \text{ feet}$$

Looking back at how I defined fractions, note that similar considerations arise when I wish to add the fractions

x and y (that is, $\frac{a}{b}, \frac{c}{d}$)

x and y (that is, $\frac{2}{3}, \frac{8}{12}$)

satisfying equations

$$b \cdot x = a$$
$$d \cdot y = c$$

$$3 \cdot x = 2$$
$$12 \cdot y = 8$$

I certainly have

$$b \cdot x + d \cdot y = a + c$$

$$3 \cdot x + 12 \cdot y = 2 + 8$$

However, this does not necessarily lead to an expression for $(x + y)$ unless $b = d$. In such a case,

$$b \cdot x + b \cdot y = a + c$$

or

$$b \cdot (x + y) = a + c$$

which, in our usual notation for fractions, is represented as

$$\frac{a}{b} + \frac{c}{d} = \frac{a + c}{b}$$

However, when $b \neq d$, I must convert these quantities into equivalent units. To do this, I proceed as follows: I multiply the expression for x by d and the expression for y by b.

$$d \cdot b \cdot x = d \cdot a$$
$$b \cdot d \cdot y = b \cdot c$$

$$12 \cdot 3 \cdot x = 12 \cdot 2$$
$$3 \cdot 12 \cdot y = 3 \cdot 8$$

As we have previously noted, this amounts to converting x and y to equivalent fractions with the unit (or denominator) of $b \cdot d$. Adding yields

$$d \cdot b \cdot x - b \cdot d \cdot y = d \cdot a - b \cdot c \qquad \boxed{12 \cdot 3 \cdot x - 3 \cdot 12 \cdot y = 12 \cdot 2 + 3 \cdot 8}$$

or

$$d \cdot b \cdot (x + y) = d \cdot a + b \cdot c \qquad \boxed{12 \cdot 3 \cdot (x + y) = 12 \cdot 2 + 3 \cdot 8}$$

In this case, I write in our usual notation

$$\frac{a}{b} + \frac{c}{d} = \frac{d \cdot a + b \cdot c}{d \cdot b} \qquad \boxed{\frac{2}{3} + \frac{8}{12} = \frac{12 \cdot 2 + 3 \cdot 8}{3 \cdot 12}}$$

The quantity $d \cdot b$ is called a *common denominator*. That is, there are integers u and v (in this case, $u = d$ and $v = b$) such that

$$b \cdot u = d \cdot b \qquad \boxed{3 \cdot \underline{12} = 36}$$
$$d \cdot v = d \cdot b \qquad \boxed{12 \cdot \underline{3} = 36}$$

However, $d \cdot b$ may not be the *least* common denominator. For example, if I want to add $\frac{1}{6}$ and $\frac{1}{4}$, a common denominator is $6 \cdot 4 = 24$ and I have

$$\begin{aligned} \frac{1}{6} + \frac{1}{4} &= \frac{4}{24} + \frac{6}{24} \\ &= \frac{10}{24} \\ &= \frac{5}{12} \end{aligned}$$

However, I can also write

$$\begin{aligned} \frac{1}{6} + \frac{1}{4} &= \frac{2}{12} + \frac{3}{12} \\ &= \frac{5}{12} \end{aligned}$$

where 12 is the *least* common denominator.[11]

What is the *least* common denominator? In practical terms, it is the smallest positive number m such that

$$\frac{a}{b} = \frac{s}{m} \quad \text{and} \quad \frac{c}{d} = \frac{t}{m} \qquad (s \text{ and } t \text{ whole numbers})$$

In what follows, I will denote the least common denominator of the fractions $\frac{a}{b} + \frac{c}{d}$ by $[b, d]$. It turns out that the least common denominator $[b, d]$ and the greatest common divisor D have much in common. That is,

$$[b, d] = \frac{b \cdot d}{D} \qquad\qquad\qquad (E)$$

---

[11] Note that $2 \cdot 6 = 12$ and $3 \cdot 4 = 12$.

Proof: Since D is the greatest common divisor, I can write b and d in the form

$$b = k_1 \cdot D \qquad\qquad \text{(Fa)}$$
$$d = k_2 \cdot D \qquad\qquad \text{(Fb)}$$

for positive integers k_1 and k_2. Thus

$$\frac{b \cdot d}{D} = k_1 \cdot d$$

$$\frac{b \cdot d}{D} = k_2 \cdot b$$

so by definition, $\frac{b \cdot d}{D}$ is a common divisor.

Now I need to show that $\frac{b \cdot d}{D}$ is the least common divisor. Assume it is not. Then

$$\frac{b \cdot d}{D} = q \cdot [b, d] + r, \qquad 0 \le r < [b, d]$$

for $q > 1$. Since $\frac{b \cdot d}{D}$ and $[b, d]$ are, by virtue of being common denominators, both divisible by b and d, it follows that the remainder r is also divisible by b and d. Since $[b, d]$ is the smallest common denominator—that is, the least possible number for which this is so—this implies that $r = 0$, and hence, $[b, d]$ divides $\frac{b \cdot d}{D}$. That is,

$$k_1 \cdot d = q \cdot [b, d] \qquad\qquad \text{(Ga)}$$
$$= q \cdot r_2 \cdot d$$
$$k_2 \cdot b = q \cdot [b, d] \qquad\qquad \text{(Gb)}$$
$$= q \cdot r_1 \cdot b$$

because $[b, d]$ is a common denominator and, by definition,

$$[b, d] = r_1 b$$
$$[b, d] = r_2 b$$

for positive integers r_1 and r_2.

Factoring out the d and b, respectively, in (G) gives

$$k_1 = q \cdot r_2$$
$$k_2 = q \cdot r_1$$

and hence, from (F),

$$b = q \cdot r_2 \cdot D$$
$$d = q \cdot r_1 \cdot D$$

Thus b and d have the factor $q \cdot D$ in common. This is a contradiction, because D is the greatest common divisor. Hence

$$[b, d] = \frac{b \cdot d}{D}$$

P R O B L E M   7 . 6

I showed previously that the greatest common divisor of the numbers 76,084 and 63,020 is 92. What is the least common denominator of the fractions of $\frac{25}{76,084}$ and $\frac{37}{63,020}$?

Fraction Multiplication and Division Algorithms

The algorithms for multiplication and division of fractions follow somewhat naturally from those used for whole numbers. Say I need to determine the product xy, where

$$x = \frac{a}{b}, y = \frac{c}{d}$$

$$x = \frac{2}{3}, y = \frac{8}{12}$$

Now

$$b \cdot x = a$$
$$d \cdot y = c$$

$$3 \cdot x = 2$$
$$12 \cdot y = 8$$

Multiplying these equations gives

$$d \cdot y \cdot b \cdot x = c \cdot a$$

$$12 \cdot y \cdot 3 \cdot x = 8 \cdot 2$$

and some rearrangement gives

$$d \cdot b \cdot (x \cdot y) = c \cdot a$$

$$12 \cdot 3 \cdot (x \cdot y) = 8 \cdot 2$$

That is,

$$x \cdot y = \frac{a \cdot c}{b \cdot d}$$

$$x \cdot y = \frac{2 \cdot 8}{3 \cdot 12}$$

Thus computation of the product of two fractions is fairly straightforward; however, it may not be entirely obvious what all this means. If I were considering the product of whole numbers—say 3 times 4—I might explain this as three groups of four. If I were multiplying—say $\frac{1}{3}$ times 3—I might explain it as taking $\frac{1}{3}$ of 3 or, equivalently, dividing 3 into three groups and taking one of them. How about $\frac{2}{3}$ of 3? This I might explain as dividing 3 into three groups and taking 2 of those groups.

So how about the product of $\frac{5}{8}$ and $\frac{7}{12}$? This I might explain as dividing $\frac{7}{12}$ into 8 groups and taking 5 of them. To illustrate, let's say I divide, so as to represent $\frac{7}{12}$, the rectangle that follows into 12 parts and shade 7 of them.

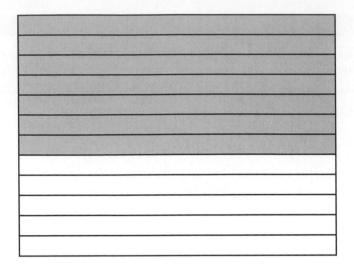

Now I take $\frac{5}{8}$ by dividing the rectangle into 8 parts and taking 5 of them.

Note that $\frac{7}{12} \cdot \frac{5}{8} = \frac{35}{96}$ and that, in the above array, a single cell is a 96th of the total and I have taken 35 of them.

P R O B L E M   7 . 7

Use the array model in computing $\frac{1}{3}$ times $\frac{3}{7}$.

Before deriving the standard algorithm for fraction division, let's think through what it means to divide one number—say 6—by another—say 2. In a sense it means to find how many groups of 2 there are in 6. How about $\frac{3}{4}$ divided by $\frac{1}{2}$? Using the same logic, I am asking, "How many groups of $\frac{1}{2}$ are there in $\frac{3}{4}$?" Well, how many groups of $\frac{1}{2}$ *are* there in $\frac{3}{4}$? Consider the following graphical approach. The top bar is divided into fourths and I have, in time-honored fashion, shaded three of them. The bottom bar is divided into halves and I have shaded one of them.

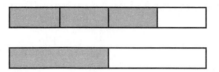

I can see 1 group of $\frac{1}{2}$ with $\frac{1}{4}$ left over, and that $\frac{1}{4}$ is $\frac{1}{2}$ of a group of $\frac{1}{2}$. Thus there are $1\frac{1}{2}$ groups of $\frac{1}{2}$ in $\frac{3}{4}$.

Another way to look at all this is from the perspective of Egyptian division:[12]

$$1 \text{ times } \frac{1}{2} = \frac{1}{2} \qquad (\text{I now have a remainder of } \tfrac{1}{4}.)$$

$$\frac{1}{2} \text{ times } \frac{1}{2} = \frac{1}{4}$$

Adding these gives the quotient of $1\frac{1}{2}$.

P R O B L E M   7 . 8

Use the graphical method to compute (a) $1\frac{1}{4}$ divided by $\frac{1}{2}$ and (b) $1\frac{1}{2}$ divided by $\frac{3}{4}$.

Now for the standard algorithm: I apply the usual definition of division, although there will be no need (as I have indicated in the examples) for a remainder term. I wish to determine q, where

$$x = q \cdot y \tag{H}$$

and

$$x = \frac{a}{b}, y = \frac{c}{d} \qquad\qquad \boxed{x = \frac{2}{3}, y = \frac{8}{12}}$$

As usual, I have

$$b \cdot x = a \qquad\qquad \boxed{3 \cdot x = 3} \tag{Ia}$$

$$d \cdot y = c \qquad\qquad \boxed{12 \cdot y = 8} \tag{Ib}$$

---

[12] It is quite possible that the Egyptians did not do something like this

Multiplying both sides of (H) by $b \cdot d$ gives

$$b \cdot d \cdot x = b \cdot d \cdot q \cdot y$$

$$3 \cdot 12 \cdot x = 3 \cdot 12 \cdot q \cdot y$$

and rearranging yields

$$d \cdot (b \cdot x) = b \cdot q \cdot (d \cdot y)$$

$$12 \cdot (3 \cdot x) = 3 \cdot q \cdot (12y)$$

Substituting the expressions for $b \cdot x$ and $d \cdot y$ from (I) gives

$$d \cdot a = b \cdot q \cdot c$$

$$12 \cdot 2 = 3 \cdot q \cdot 8$$

and rearranging yields

$$b \cdot c \cdot q = a \cdot d$$

$$3 \cdot 8 \cdot q = 2 \cdot 12$$

That is, the fraction q—the quotient—is

$$\frac{a \cdot d}{b \cdot c}$$

$$\frac{2 \cdot 2}{3 \cdot 8}$$

or the product of the fractions $\frac{a}{b}$ and $\frac{d}{c}$.

The fraction $\frac{d}{c}$ is called the *reciprocal* of the fraction $\frac{c}{d}$. To see this, note that, using the definition of fraction, $\frac{d}{c}$ is the solution to the equation.

$$c \cdot z = d$$

just as $\frac{c}{d}$ is a solution to the equation

$$d \cdot y = c$$

Multiplying these two equations gives

$$c \cdot d \cdot (y \cdot z) = c \cdot d$$

and dividing by $c \cdot d$ on both sides gives

$$y \cdot z = 1$$

That is, $z = \frac{d}{c}$ is the inverse, or reciprocal, of $y = \frac{c}{d}$.

⚔ Ratios and Proportionality

Notions about ratios and proportions go back to Euclid and earlier. In the time of Euclid, expressions of the form $a:b$ were used to name ratios. Today we use the representation $\frac{a}{b}$ to name ratios as well as fractions. What is a ratio? The definition I'll use here[13] follows.

---

[13] Much of what I discuss here is taken from John P. Smith, The development of students' knowledge of fractions and ratios. In *Making Sense of Fractions, Ratios, and Proportions*, ed. Bonnie Litwiller and George Bright (Reston, VA: NCTM, 2002).

A ratio is a relational number that has two properties: (1) it relates two quantities in one situation, and (2) it projects that relationship onto a second situation in which the relative amounts of the two quantities remain the same.

For example, suppose a soccer team scores 11 goals in 5 games. Someone might use the ratio "11 goals, 5 games" to estimate how many goals the team would score in a 15-game season (that is, 33 goals, 15 games). The first property is exemplified by *scoring in 5 games,* and the second property is exemplified by *scoring by the end of the season.* Thus thinking about a ratio is equivalent to what is often called *proportional reasoning,* with one important exception. Proportional reasoning is a kind of thinking; it is not a matter of writing a particular expression down on paper.

Ratios have a multiplicative structure. Thinking with a ratio in the context of the soccer season involves replicating the 11 goals across each group of 5 games. For example,

11 goals, 5 games   11 goals, 5 games   11 goals, 5 games

or

33 goals, 15 games

When there are many such situations in which the quantities stand in the same multiplicative relationship, thinking about a ratio is equivalent to thinking about the function

$$f(x) = \frac{11}{5} \cdot x$$

where the domain is games played and the range is number of goals.

Certain precursors for ratio appear in the pre-K years. It seems that pre-K children have intuitive notions of scale (two *large* objects on the table belong together) and of covariation (if one of two matched objects changes in size, the other must also. These precursors appear to support the later development of sensible strategies in proportional situations.[14]

In the upper elementary grades—usually in the sixth grade—children are often exposed to problems of the form[15]

> A restaurant sets tables by putting 7 pieces of silverware and 4 pieces of china on each placemat. If it used 35 pieces of silverware in its table settings last night, how many pieces of china did it use?

or

> I can purchase 1 pound of candy for $1.20. How many pounds can I purchase for $1.80?

---

[14] Smith, p. 15.
[15] Smith, p. 15.

In their solution of the china problem, students typically increment the set of 4 pieces of china the same number of times as they increment the set of silverware (that is, 5 times, to reach 20 pieces of china). Such strategy can be executed by skip-counting or by saying each ordered pair, thus effectively building up larger quantities of silver and china from the combined unit, *7 silver and 4 china*.

Historically and at present, solutions to such problems can also be computed by using the Rule of Three, the method of finding the fourth term of a mathematical proportion when the first three terms are known, and where the first term is in proportion to the second as the third term is to the unknown fourth. For instance, in the candy problem, $1.20 is to 1 pound of candy as $1.80 is to the unknown amount of candy. The technique for computing the fourth term—the *missing* term—is to multiply the second and third terms and then divide their product by the first term. For instance,

$$\frac{1 \text{ pound}}{\$1.20} \cdot \$1.80 = 1\frac{1}{2} \text{ pounds of candy}$$

The solution technique is somewhat straightforward—I'll discuss why it works shortly—but children find it difficult to learn or resist using it when they do learn it. It is unclear whether they find the notion difficult to link to their early knowledge of ratio or that it does not match the mental operations involved in the *building-up* strategy. (What, after all, is one "pound-dollar," let alone $1.80 of them?)

Why does the solution technique work? It works simply because we have two ratios—for instance, the before and after—that we wish to be equivalent. If we represent the first by $\frac{a}{b}$ and the second by $\frac{n}{c}$, where n is unknown, then we have from (A) that

$$a \cdot c = b \cdot n$$

or

$$n = \frac{ac}{b}$$

That is, we *cross-multiply*.

P R O B L E M   7 . 9

Consider the following currency chart:

$$\$1.00 \text{ US} = \$1.60 \text{ Canadian}$$
$$\$1.00 \text{ US} = 1.30 \text{ euros}$$

a. Convert $500 Canadian dollars to U.S. currency.
b. Convert $500 Canadian dollars to euros.

Investigations

1. Jessica suggests to you that a reasonably efficient method for approximating $\sqrt{2}$—which is approximately 1.414214—is
   a. Choose two fractions $\frac{a}{b}$ and $\frac{c}{d}$ $\left(\frac{a}{b} < \frac{c}{d}\right)$ whose product is 2. [I'll choose, for example, $\frac{1}{2}$ and $\frac{4}{1}$.]
   b. Compute the mediant by adding the numerators and denominators $\frac{a+c}{b+d}$. [I get for my example $\frac{5}{3}$.]
   c. Choose another fraction $\frac{e}{f}$ so that $\left(\frac{a+c}{b+d}\right) \cdot \frac{e}{f} = 2$. [For my example, I'll choose $\frac{6}{5}$.]
   d. Repeat steps b and c until the desired accuracy is reached. [For my example, $\frac{6}{5} = 1.2$, and the next few calculations give $\frac{16}{11} = 1.454545$; $\frac{38}{27} = 1.407407$; $\frac{92}{65} = 1.415384$.]

   You are a bit skeptical about this and ask Jessica whether it always works. Jessica says she is fairly sure that it does, but to prove it she needs to prove that $\frac{a}{b} < \frac{a+c}{b+d} < \frac{c}{d}$ is true for any two fractions such that $\frac{a}{b} < \frac{c}{d}$. Give Jessica a hand and prove that this inequality holds.[16]

2. Tony approaches you after class. "Mr. Talman," he says, "LaShawn and I have been wondering about $\frac{16}{64}$. I say you can prove that

$$\frac{16}{64} = \frac{1}{4}$$

   by canceling the 6s. LaShawn says that $\frac{16}{64}$ does equal $\frac{1}{4}$, but you can't prove it that way. Who's right?" I, of course, tell Tony he is wrong and give him a counterexample. "How about $\frac{19}{95}$?" Tony thinks for a minute and says, "But Mr. Talman, that's right!" Now I've got a problem. How many two-digit fractions such as this, aside from the trivial ones like $\frac{22}{22}$, are there anyway? [*Hint:* You are interested in fractions of the form $\frac{10a+b}{10b+c}$ such that

$$\frac{10a+b}{10b+c} = \frac{a}{c}$$

   and $a < c, b$. If you simplify this equation by cross-multiplying, you get

$$9ac + bc = 10ab$$

   Use this equation with the fact that $a, b,$ and c are positive digits to determine the possible values for $a, b,$ and c.]

3. Prove that the sum of the reciprocals of the divisors of N is

$$\frac{\sigma(N)}{N}$$

   where $\sigma(N)$ is the sum of the factors of N. [*Hint:* The least common divisor of these divisors will be N. You may also wish to refer to Investigation 2 of Chapter 5.]

---

[16] This is, in a sense, a simplification of the root extraction technique discussed by Domingo León Gómez Morín in his *The Fifth Arithmetical Operation* (see http://mipagina.cantv.net/arithmetic/index.htm). If, as Morín indicates, you begin with three fractions which multiply to 2 and compute the pairwise mediants at each step, the approximation converges significantly faster.

4. You ask a fourth grader whether the following statement is true:

$$\frac{5}{3} = 1\frac{2}{3}$$

The fourth grader immediately says, "Yes," and when you ask why, she says, "Well, 5 times 3 is 15 (referring to the left-hand side) and $2 + 3$ is 5 (referring to the right-hand side), so you have 15 equal to 15." How many instances of this are there? And what are they? Here is a counterexample:

$$\frac{7}{3} = 1\frac{1}{3}$$

but 21 is not equal to 24.

Decimals

In this chapter you and I will consider the art and practice of decimal arithmetic. In particular, we will explore the mathematics behind such calculations as

$$
\begin{array}{r}
123.52 \\
\times \quad 23.6 \\
\hline
74112 \\
37056 \\
24704 \\
\hline
2915.072
\end{array}
$$

I will focus primarily on terminating, or finite, decimal expansions—that is, decimal numbers with a finite number of digits. However, because decimal arithmetic was largely introduced for the purpose of simplifying calculations involving rational numbers, you and I will examine the relationship between a certain class of infinite, or nonterminating, decimal expansions and the rational numbers. One member of this class, the rational number $\frac{1}{3}$, has, for example, the nonterminating decimal expansion

$$.333333333333 \ldots \quad \text{or} \quad .\overline{3}$$

Such infinite decimal expansions, intriguingly, bring the rationals (discussed in the preceding chapter) face to face with the reals (the subject of the chapter that follows).

✖ Decimals from a Historical Perspective

More than a thousand years intervened between the discovery that one could represent all whole numbers in a base-10 system with nine symbols and a zero and the extension of such ideas to decimal fractions. In a certain sense, there was no need for such an innovation as approximations to square, and cube roots, when needed, were given in terms of the Babylonian sexagesimal system of fractions. For instance, it was known in approximately 1900 BC that

$$\sqrt{2} \approx 1 + \frac{24}{60} + \frac{51}{60^2} + \frac{10}{60^3}$$

In the fourteenth century, however, Johannis de Muris gave the square root of 2 as 1.41.4, saying that the 1 represented units, the first 4 tenths, the second

1 "tenths of tenths," and the second 4 "tenths of tenths of tenths."[1] He later extended this, writing the result also to twentieths of twentieths of twentieths, finally giving the result in sexagesimal fractions.[2]

It appears that special rules for division by integral multiples of 10, 100, and so on led to an actual decimal point in one problem in a treatise by Francesco Pellizzati in 1492, and Christian Rudolf, in the first half of the sixteenth century, used decimal fractions in computing compound interest. However, the first systematic discussion of decimal fractions was given by Simon Stevin in 1585. This work was addressed to astronomers, surveyors, masters of money (of the mint), and all merchants. Stevin says of this work that it treats of "something so simple, that it hardly merits the name of invention." He adds,

> We will speak freely of the great utility of this invention; I say great, much
> greater than I judge any of you will suspect, and this without at all exalting
> my own opinion. . . . For the astronomer knows the difficult multiplications
> and divisions which proceed from the progression with degrees, minutes,
> seconds and thirds . . . [and] the surveyor, he will recognize the great benefit
> which the world would receive from this science, to avoid . . . the tiresome
> multiplications in Verges, feet and often inches, which are notably awkward,
> and often the cause of error. The same of the masters of the mint, merchants,
> and others. . . . But the more that these things mentioned are worth while,
> and the ways to achieve them more laborious, the greater still is this
> discovery disme [dime], which removes all these difficulties. But how? It
> teaches (to tell much in one word) to compute easily, without fractions,
> all computations which are encountered in the affairs of human beings, in
> such a way that the four principles of arithmetic which are called addition,
> subtraction, multiplication and division, are able to achieve this end, causing
> also similar facility to those who use the casting-board.[3] Now if by this
> means will be gained precious time; if by this means labor, annoyance, error,
> damage, and other accidents commonly joined with these computations, be
> avoided, then I submit this plan voluntarily to your judgment.[4]

By the eighteenth century, the utility of decimal fractions had been demonstrated so clearly that the treatment of this subject was regularly taken up in arithmetic texts of that time. English texts of the early eighteenth century commonly provided an extensive treatment of the decimal arithmetic. The American texts of the eighteenth century included full discussion of decimals, using the word *separatrix* to designate the decimal point.

☜ Decimals from a Developmental Perspective

In most U.S. elementary schools, children first encounter decimal numbers in the fourth grade, although their use in extensive calculations begins in the fifth grade. By this time, most children are proficient with simple whole-number

---

[1] Louis Charles Karpinski, *The History of Arithmetic* (Chicago: Rand McNally, 1925), pp. 129–130.
[2] $\sqrt{2}$ was obtained by writing 2,000,000, taking the square root of this, dividing by 1000 (since $\sqrt{2,000,000} = \sqrt{2} \cdot \sqrt{1,000,000}$ and $\sqrt{1,000,000} = 1000$), and reducing the result to sexagesimal fractions. This particular method appears in manuscripts of the twelfth century and in printed books of the sixteenth century.
[3] This board, together with markers or counters, was used much as an abacus.
[4] Quoted in Karpinski, p. 131.

computations and possess significant conceptual and procedural knowledge that can, with appropriate instruction, contribute to their learning of decimal arithmetic.

The decimal number system is nonetheless a complex representation system. The earlier systems of whole numbers and common fractions have, as Sevin foresaw, become subsumed into a single system that is quite elegant and efficient. Some advantages are that arithmetic within a decimal number system is built, to a degree, on those concepts and procedures already encountered within a base-10 number system. It also avoids some of the perceived awkwardness of the rationals.

This advance, however, has a price. It appears that children often recognize few, if any, connections between their conceptual knowledge of decimal fractions and the procedures they use in decimal arithmetic. The absence of such links can be so extensive and pervasive that it is as though the two kinds of knowledge belong to two separate mental worlds.[5] It is not unusual, for example, for children erroneously to attempt to overgeneralize the rules they memorized for the whole-number arithmetic operations. Consider the scenario that follows.

> Ms. Stowe's fifth grade class has been working with decimals. Although her class has discussed how to represent decimals, they have not discussed how to add them. As an introductory lesson, she has designed the following problem:

>> Pretend you are a jeweler. Sometimes people come in to get rings resized. When you cut down a ring to make it smaller, you keep the small portion of gold in exchange for the work you have done. Recently you have collected these amounts:

>> 1.14 grams, .089 gram, and .3 gram

>> Now you have a repair job to do for which you need some gold. You are wondering if you have enough. Work together with your group to figure out how much gold you have collected. Be prepared to show the class your solution.

> Ms. Stowe circulates among the working students. She stops to listen to Jeanine, Paul, and Steve. Jeanine looks up and says, "We could line the numbers up on the right like you do with other numbers." Paul adds, "Maybe we should line up the decimals, but I don't know why we would do that." Ms. Stowe replies, "I think you're suggesting that you might line this problem up differently from the way you line up whole-number addition. Is that right?" Paul nods. Ms. Stowe continues, "Why do you line whole numbers up the way you do? What's the reason for it?" Paul looks puzzled. "I don't know. It's just the way you do it. That's how we learned to do it." Steve says quietly, "I think it would help if we drew a picture, like of the base-10 blocks."

---

[5] Diana Wearne and James Hiebert, Constructing and using meaning for mathematical symbols: The case of decimal fractions. In *Number Concepts and Operations in the Middle Grades,* ed. James Hiebert and Merlyn Behr (Mahwah, NJ: Erlbaum, 1988), p. 220.

After the groups finished their work, the class as a whole had a discussion. Eric reported that the students in his group represented the problem as follows:

$$\begin{array}{rl} 1 & \\ .3 & \text{gram} \\ 1.14 & \text{grams} \\ +.089 & \text{gram} \\ \hline 1.529 & \text{grams} \end{array}$$

Paul immediately asks Eric why they decided to line up the numbers that way, and Eric responded that the group thought that, just as with whole-number addition, they needed to line up the tenths with the tenths and the hundredths with the hundredths to "make it come out right."

Decimal Arithmetic

Operations with finite decimal numbers—for example, numbers of the form 1.14—are fairly straightforward if we keep in mind that 1.14 is the mixed number

$$1.14 = 1 + \frac{1}{10} + \frac{4}{100}$$

or, in expanded notation,

$$1.14 = 1 \cdot 10^0 + 1 \cdot 10^{-1} + 4 \cdot 10^{-2}$$

Note that the value of such fractions is preserved in the way they are spoken. That is, .1 is said as "one-tenth" and .01 is said as "one-hundredth." As with the use of the term *borrow* in subtraction, saying "point zero one," unfortunately, destroys this natural association.

PROBLEM 8.1

How would you say the number .000001? (b) the number .0000031?

Decimal Addition and Subtraction

When we keep in mind what decimals are, the rules for arithmetic are fairly simple. That is, we add numbers with similar denominators (or, for example, represented by like powers of 10). Thus, if I wish to add .3, 1.14, and .089, I proceed, in effect, as follows:

$$\begin{aligned} .3 + 1.14 + .089 &= \frac{3}{10} + \left(1 + \frac{1}{10} + \frac{4}{100}\right) + \left(\frac{8}{100} + \frac{9}{1000}\right) \\ &= 1 + \frac{3}{10} + \frac{1}{10} + \frac{4}{100} + \frac{8}{100} + \frac{9}{1000} \\ &= 1 + \frac{4}{10} + \frac{12}{100} + \frac{9}{1000} \end{aligned}$$

Decomposing yields

$$\frac{12}{100} = \frac{1}{10} + \frac{2}{100}$$

so

$$.3 + 1.14 + .089 = 1 + \frac{4}{10} + \frac{1}{10} + \frac{2}{100} + \frac{9}{1000}$$

$$= 1 + \frac{5}{10} + \frac{2}{100} + \frac{9}{1000}$$

$$= 1.529$$

Addition or subtraction can also be performed using the rules developed for whole numbers. A brief look, using expanded notation, shows the rationale. Say we wish to subtract 1.43 from 2.33. In expanded notation, we have

$$1.43 = 1 \cdot 10^0 + 4 \cdot 10^{-1} + 3 \cdot 10^{-2}$$

$$2.33 = 2 \cdot 10^0 + 3 \cdot 10^{-1} + 3 \cdot 10^{-2}$$

so

$$2.33 - 1.43 = 2 \cdot 10^0 + 3 \cdot 10^{-1} + 3 \cdot 10^{-2} - (1 \cdot 10^0 + 4 \cdot 10^{-1} + 3 \cdot 10^{-2})$$

$$= (2 \cdot 10^0 - 1 \cdot 10^0) + (3 \cdot 10^{-1} - 4 \cdot 10^{-1}) + (3 \cdot 10^{-2} - 3 \cdot 10^{-2})$$

$$= (2 \cdot 10^0 - 1 \cdot 10^0) + (3 \cdot 10^{-1} - 4 \cdot 10^{-1})$$

Because we cannot take .4 from .3, we must, as one says, *borrow* a 1 from the 2. That is,

$$2.33 - 1.43 = (1 \cdot 10^0 - 1 \cdot 10^0) + (1 \cdot 10^0 + 3 \cdot 10^{-1} - 4 \cdot 10^{-1})$$

$$= (1 \cdot 10^0 - 1 \cdot 10^0) + (13 \cdot 10^{-1} - 4 \cdot 10^{-1})$$

$$= (1 \cdot 10^0 - 1 \cdot 10^0) + 9 \cdot 10^{-1}$$

$$= 9 \cdot 10^{-1}$$

$$= .9$$

Representing all this in the usual shorthand notation gives

$$\overset{1}{2.}{}^1 33$$
$$\underline{-1.\ 43}$$
$$.\ 90$$

Decimal Multiplication and Division

Again keeping in mind that a quantity like 2.43 is a mixed number—for example, I would say 2.43 as "two and forty-three hundredths"—the rules for multiplication of decimals should make sense. Let's take a look at 2.43 times 1.43.

$$2.43 \cdot 1.43 = \frac{243}{100} \cdot \frac{143}{100}$$

$$= \frac{243 \cdot 143}{100 \cdot 100}$$

$$= \frac{34749}{10000}$$

Dividing by 10000 means we shift the number 34749 four places to the right.[6] That is,

$$10^4 \ 10^3 \ 10^2 \ 10^1 \ 10^0 \ 10^{-1} \ 10^{-2} \ 10^{-3} \ 10^{-4}$$
$$3 \quad 4 \quad 7 \quad 4 \quad 9$$

becomes

$$10^4 \ 10^3 \ 10^2 \ 10^1 \ 10^0 \ 10^{-1} \ 10^{-2} \ 10^{-3} \ 10^{-4}$$
$$3 \quad 4 \quad 7 \quad 4 \quad 9$$

Thus

$$2.43 \cdot 1.43 = 3.4749$$

or "three and four thousand, seven hundred, and forty-nine ten-thousandths."

P R O B L E M   8 . 2

(a) Why does multiplying a number by a power of 10 shift that number to the left? (b) Why does dividing a number by a power of 10 shift that number to the right? (c) How many places would a number shift to the left if you multiplied it by 10^{25}?

The rationale for division of decimals again derives from the fact that decimals are, in effect, fractions. A typical problem in an elementary school textbook might read

$$1.43\overline{)2.4}$$

for which we have the somewhat mysterious rule "Shift both decimal points two places to the right and compute the equivalent problem," which in this case is

$$143\overline{)240}$$

Let's see what is happening. Keeping in mind that we are dealing with fractions, let me write this division as the fraction problem

$$\frac{2.4}{1.43}$$

I can convert this to a nice equivalent fraction by multiplying the numerator and denominator by 100, which gives the equivalent fraction

$$\frac{2.4}{1.43} = \frac{100 \cdot 2.4}{100 \cdot 1.43}$$
$$= \frac{240}{143}$$

---

[6] Note that the decimal point (real or imagined) does not move in such instances. The decimal point is only a marker to indicate that to its right, all digits should be taken as the appropriate decimal fractions. Arcane rules for decimal movement, though well intended, cause children a great deal of difficulty, because, for positive numbers, it is sufficient to remember that multiplication by a power of 10 causes a number to get larger (the number of shifts corresponding to the power). Likewise, it is sufficient to remember that division by a power of 10 causes a number to get smaller (the number of shifts corresponding to the power). The multiplicative structure of our base-10 system is no minor matter.

which, when written in the customary notation for problems of this sort, is just

$$143\overline{)240}$$

⚹ Nonterminating Decimals

The ubiquity of the decimal system comes, however, at a price. Although fractions such as $\frac{1}{2}, \frac{1}{4}, \frac{1}{10}, \frac{1}{100}, \frac{1}{1000}$, and so on are easily represented in a base-10 decimal system, this is not the case for $\frac{1}{3}, \frac{1}{7}$, and the like, as a little decimal division shows. For example, as we have mentioned, in a base-10 decimal system,

$$\frac{1}{3} = .333333333\ldots$$

This type of nonterminating behavior does not occur in a base-3 system. We know that

$$\frac{1}{3} = 3^{-1}$$

and hence,

$$\frac{1}{3} = .1_3$$

Note, however, that in a base-3 system,

$$\frac{1}{10} = .0022002200220022\ldots_3$$

P R O B L E M   8 . 3

Write $\frac{1}{2}$ in a base-6 system.

Nonetheless, $\frac{1}{3}$ does seem to have a patterned representation in a base-10 decimal system. The 3 in .333 …, for example, repeats ad infinitum. In fact, all fractions that have a nonterminating expansion repeat. Consider $\frac{1}{7}$. Dividing yields

$$
\begin{array}{r}
.1428571 \\
7\overline{)1.0000000} \\
\underline{7} \\
30 \\
\underline{28} \\
20 \\
\underline{14} \\
60 \\
\underline{56} \\
40 \\
\underline{35} \\
50 \\
\underline{49} \\
10 \quad \leftarrow \text{The repeat begins.} \\
\underline{7} \\
3
\end{array}
$$

That is, because there are only 10 possible digits, every such fraction division must eventually repeat. Using a bar to indicate the portion that repeats, I write

$$\frac{1}{7} = .\overline{142857}$$

and $\frac{1}{3} = .\overline{3}$.

P R O B L E M   8 . 4

Give the nonterminating decimal expansions for (a) $\frac{2}{7}$; (b) $\frac{1}{3} + \frac{1}{4}$.

Two interesting mathematical questions are whether all nonterminating decimals are represented by fractions and, if not, which ones are. I'll discuss the second question here and the first in the chapter on *reals*. Consider the nonterminating repeating decimal

$$N = .44047619047619\ldots$$

Now

$$10^2 \cdot N = 44.047619047619\ldots$$

and

$$10^{(2+6)} \cdot N = 44047619.047619047619\ldots$$

so

$$10^{(2+6)} \cdot N - 10^2 \cdot N = 44047619 - 44$$

and

$$N = \frac{44047619 - 44}{10^{(2+6)} - 10^2}$$

$$= \frac{37}{84}$$

This suggests that any nonterminating decimal that shows a repeating pattern can be represented by a fraction.[7]

P R O B L E M   8 . 5

What rational numbers correspond to (a) $.\overline{6}$; (b) $.\overline{1}$; (c) $.\overline{9}$; (d) $.\overline{4321}$?

---

[7] There is a sense in which all rational numbers have a nonterminating decimal expansion. For instance, $\frac{1}{10} = .1\overline{0}$. Thus one might say that rational numbers (and this, of course, includes integers) are characterized by the fact that they have repeating nonterminating decimal expansions.

Investigations

1. In describing his experiences at a bargain sale, Smith says that half his money was gone in just 30 minutes, so that he was left with as many pennies as he had dollars before, and half as many dollars as before he had pennies. How much did he spend?[8]

2. Prove that all positive rationals N with a finite decimal expansion have the form

$$N = \frac{p}{2^\alpha \cdot 5^\beta}$$

   for p, α, β positive integers.

3. You have a lot of books in your library and it's a rainy day without anything much to do. You decide to build an arch starting at the kitchen table and extending one foot into your living room.

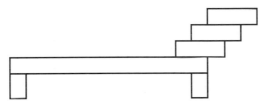

   If the books you are using are all of the same weight and approximately 8 inches long, how many books will it take? Do you think you could build an arch extending a mile? Why or why not? [*Hint:* The center of mass of an 8-inch book is at the 4-inch mark, so for the first book not to fall off the table, its center of mass should be on the table—and hence a 4-inch overhang is possible. How about the second book? Well, the second book, by the same reasoning, can overhang the first book by 4 inches. However, you need to make sure that the *net* center of mass of the two books together is on the table. Marking from the end of your arch, the center of mass of the second book is at 4 inches, and the center of mass of the first is at 8 inches, so the combined center of mass is at $\frac{8+4}{2}$, or 6 inches. This means the two books together can overhang the table by 6 inches (or $\frac{1}{2} + \frac{1}{4}$ of the length of a book). How about three books? Well, the top two books can overhang the bottommost book by 6 inches. Hence, marking from the end of your arch, the center of mass of the third book is at 4 inches, the center of mass of the second book is at 8 inches, and the center of mass of the third book is at 10 inches. Thus the combined center of mass is at $\frac{10+8+4}{3}$, or $7\frac{1}{3}$ inches (or $\frac{1}{2} + \frac{1}{4} + \frac{1}{6}$ of the length of a book). Do you see the pattern? Keep it up!]

4. As you have seen, some rational numbers have nonterminating repeating decimal patterns. An interesting question is whether one can predict just

---

[8] Sam Loyd, *Mathematical Puzzles of Sam Loyd*, ed. Martin Gardner (New York: Dover, 1959).

how long its period will be (that is, how many numbers before it repeats) without doing all the division. Prove the following:

The decimal expansion of an irreducible rational number $\frac{m}{n}$ begins after s terms and has a period of t, where s and t are the smallest numbers such that

$$10^s \equiv 10^{s+t} \pmod{n}$$

For example,

$10^0 \equiv 1 \pmod{84}$	$10^1 \equiv 10 \pmod{84}$	$10^2 \equiv \underline{16} \pmod{84}$
$10^3 \equiv -8 \pmod{84}$	$10^4 \equiv 4 \pmod{84}$	$10^5 \equiv 40 \pmod{84}$
$10^6 \equiv 20 \pmod{84}$	$10^7 \equiv -32 \pmod{84}$	$10^8 \equiv \underline{16} \pmod{84}$

Hint: Return to and examine the example I did in the previous section. Note that I had

$$\frac{37}{84} = \frac{44047619 - 44}{10^{(2+6)} - 10^2}$$

Real Numbers

The term *real number* refers to those numbers that are possible outcomes of measurement. Hence, it excludes numbers termed imaginary or complex, such as numbers that satisfy an equation of the form

$$x^2 + 1 = 0$$

Thus, real numbers include the whole or natural numbers, the integers, and the rationals (remember too that the natural numbers are contained within the integers, and the integers are contained within the natural numbers).

My focus in this chapter will be on the art and practice of real number arithmetic or, one might say, the mathematics of measurement. If you think about it, you might wonder at the contents of such a chapter. You and I have already discussed the arithmetic of decimals, and it seems that with sophisticated measurement instruments and techniques, one could always exactly express the length of a line, for example, by a rational number (which, of course, includes those numbers that have a finite decimal expansion). However, as has been known from antiquity, there are simple measurements that cannot be made with the numbers you and I have examined so far. Consider the following diagram:

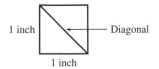

which represents a square with 1-inch sides. This is a diagram that we could, in principle, draw reasonably precisely. However, the length of the diagonal is $\sqrt{2}$ inches, a number that falls into none of the numeric categories I have mentioned previously. This is a number to which we give the name *irrational*,[1] and as you might suspect, it can be represented only by a *nonrepeating* nonterminating decimal.

Let me stress this perhaps disturbing fact.[2] There are numbers that are not expressible with our base-10 notation. I may well determine the ten-thousandths digit in the expansion of $\sqrt{2}$. This does not mean I know or can even predict the

---

[1] That is, not represented by a rational.
[2] The realization that such a simple construction leads to such incommensurability is said to have precipitated a crisis in Greek mathematics. However, this may be more myth than fact.

twenty-thousandths digit. How do I know this? I'll show that $\sqrt{2}$ is irrational. This will be a proof by *contradiction*.

I'll begin by assuming the contrary: by assuming that $\sqrt{2}$ is rational. That is,

$$\sqrt{2} = \frac{a}{b}$$

where a and b are positive whole numbers and the fraction $\frac{a}{b}$ is reduced to its lowest terms (that is, a and b have no common factor)[3] and then show that this leads to a contradiction. Thus I will have shown that it cannot be the case that $\sqrt{2}$ is a rational number.

Proof: I have assumed that $\sqrt{2} = \frac{a}{b}$. I'll square both sides, which gives

$$2 = \left(\frac{a}{b}\right)^2$$

$$= \frac{a^2}{b^2}$$

Multiplying both sides by b^2 gives

$$2 \cdot b^2 = a^2 \qquad\qquad (A)$$

Now 2 divides the left side of the equation (A) and thus 2 divides the right side. That is, a^2 is even. How about a? Well, a is certainly either even or odd. If it were odd, then, because an odd number times an odd number is odd, a^2 would be odd. Thus a must be even, and I can write a in the form $2 \cdot n$ for some positive integer n.

I'm going to substitute $2 \cdot n$ for a in (A), which gives

$$2 \cdot b^2 = (2 \cdot n)^2$$

Expanding what is in the parentheses gives

$$2 \cdot b^2 = (2)^2 \cdot n^2$$

$$= 4 \cdot n^2$$

and dividing by 2 on both sides gives

$$b^2 = 2 \cdot n^2 \qquad\qquad (B)$$

Note the similarity between (A) and (B). I can use a similar argument to show that b equals $2 \cdot m$ for some positive integer m.

P R O B L E M   9 . 1

Prove that $b = 2 \cdot m$ for some positive integer m.

---

[3] If you have concerns about this condition, remember that in practice, it can always be done.

Thus a and b are both even and, hence, both divisible by 2. However, this contradicts my assumption that the fraction $\frac{a}{b}$ is reduced to its lowest terms. Thus, $\sqrt{2}$ is *not* a rational number.

We examined the arithmetic of terminating decimals earlier, so let's focus primarily on the "arithmetic of the irrationals"—and thus on the issue of how one does arithmetic with uncertain measurements. Along the way, we will also touch on the Pythagorean Theorem:

The sum of the squares of the two sides of a right triangle is equal to the square of the hypotenuse.

And I will illustrate how certain irrational numbers can be represented in a *predictable* fashion as continued fractions. As a case in point,

$$\sqrt{2} = 1 + \cfrac{1}{2 + \cfrac{1}{2 + \cfrac{1}{2 + \cdots}}}$$

❊ The Reals from a Historical Perspective

There are other irrationals. Among those of historical importance are the ratio of the circumference of a circle to its radius, π; the Golden Ratio, $\varphi = \frac{1 + \sqrt{5}}{2}$; and the base of the natural logarithms,[4] $e = \Sigma_{n=0}^{\infty} \frac{1}{n!}$. However, in this brief survey we will focus on $\sqrt{2}$ and π, which commonly come up in the elementary school curriculum.

Pi: π

That the ratio of the circumference of a circle to its radius is a constant has been known throughout recorded history. We can find approximations, probably derived through measurement, in the records of many ancient civilizations. For example, the earliest known value for π that was used in China, as far back as the twelfth century BC, was 3. There is good evidence that the value $4\left(\frac{8}{9}\right)^2$, or approximately 3.16, was used in Egypt around 1650 BC. In India (around AD 628), Brahmagupta used three values of π: 3 for rough work; $\sqrt{10}$ for *neat* work; and, for closer accuracy, the value of $3\frac{177}{1250}$ given by Aryabhata around AD 499.

One of the first recorded theoretical derivations for π was given by Archimedes (287–212 BC). He showed that

$$\frac{223}{71} < \pi < \frac{22}{7}$$

---

[4] The factorial is defined as follows: $0! = 1$, $1! = 1$, $2! = 2 \cdot 1, \ldots, n! = n(n-1)(n-2) \cdots 2 \cdot 1$. Thus, because Σ indicates the summation of terms, $e = \frac{1}{0!} + \frac{1}{1!} + \frac{1}{2!} + \cdots + \frac{1}{n!} + \cdots$.

His approach was roughly as follows. If a circle is enclosed between two regular polygons of n sides (for example, two squares, two regular pentagons, or two regular hexagons),

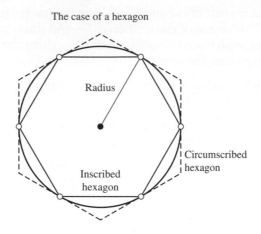

The case of a hexagon

Radius

Circumscribed
hexagon

Inscribed
hexagon

then, as the number of sides increases, the gap between the circumference of the circle and the perimeters of these polygons decreases, the result being that for n very large, the circumference of the circle is essentially equal to the perimeter of the polygons. Since Archimedes could, in theory, derive the formula for the perimeter of a regular inscribed polygon (the polygon within) or a regular circumscribed polygon (the polygon outside) for a radius r, he could theoretically compute the ratio of perimeter to radius and obtain an approximation for π.[5] In the case of a hexagon, the inner ratio is 3 and the outer ratio is approximately 3.46.

As time passed, better approximations—a quest driven in part by measurement needs in astronomy and building—were obtained for π. Some milestones were al-Kushi (about AD 1430) determining π correctly to 14 digits, Van Cuelen (about AD 1600) correctly to 35 digits, Sharp (1699) to 71 digits, and Rutherford (1853) to 440 digits. At present we know π to more than 10^{12} digits.

Square Root of 2: $\sqrt{2}$

Approximation of the square root of 2 is a little more tractable, so its history is somewhat different. It appears that the Babylonians as early as 2000 BC had tables of approximations of both square and cube roots. In one famous clay tablet identified as YBC 7289, there is evidence that $\sqrt{2}$ was known to be approximately 1.41421297. It is not clear what method was employed to obtain such a result; however, it may have been somewhat similar to the following:

I'm going to begin by approximating $\sqrt{10}$ by the largest possible integer I can. That is 3. Now $\sqrt{10} > 3$, so $\frac{\sqrt{10}}{3} > 1$. However, if $\frac{\sqrt{10}}{3} > 1$, then

$$\sqrt{10}\,\frac{\sqrt{10}}{3} > \sqrt{10}$$

<hr/>

[5] Archimedes stopped at a regular polygon of 96 sides.

so

$$\frac{10}{3} > \sqrt{10}$$

A picture of these inequalities, then, is

$$\frac{10}{3} > \sqrt{10} > 3$$

This suggests that somewhere within the interval between $\frac{10}{3}$ and 3, there is a better estimate for $\sqrt{10}$. A good choice for such an estimate is essentially the midpoint of that interval:

$$a = \frac{3 + \frac{10}{3}}{2}$$

$$\approx 3.167$$

A bit of algebra shows that

$$\frac{10}{a} < \sqrt{10} < a$$

and I can continue my approximations as before, with narrower and narrower intervals.[6] For example, a better approximation would be[7]

$$\frac{a + \frac{10}{a}}{2} \approx 3.16228$$

P R O B L E M   9 . 2

Determine the next two approximations for $\sqrt{10}$.

Around 390 BC, Theon gave another method of approximating square roots:

> When we seek a square root, we take first the root of the nearest square number. We then double this and divide with it the remainder reduced to minutes, and subtract the square of the quotient; then we reduce the remainder by seconds and divide by twice the degrees and minutes. We thus obtain nearly the root of the quadratic.[8]

Sounds complicated, doesn't it? The method is based on a result[9] of Euclid:

$$(a + b)^2 = a^2 + 2ab + b^2$$

---

[6] Note that $a \cdot \frac{10}{a} = 10$. Hence, this method of approximation has somewhat the same behavior as the root extraction techniques discussed by Domingo León Gómez Morín in his *The Fifth Arithmetical Operation* (see http://mipagina.cantv.net/arithmetic/index.htm).
[7] The square root of 10 is approximately 3.162278.
[8] David Eugene Smith, *History of Mathematics: Special Topics of Elementary Mathematics* (New York: Dover, 1925), p. 145.
[9] This result appears to have been known considerably before Euclid recorded it.

That is, if we square the sum of two numbers, the result is the square of the first plus two times the product of the numbers plus the square of the second.

I'll sketch a somewhat modern rationale for this technique,[10] using $\sqrt{10}$ as an example.

Because the largest square less than 10 is 9, I write

$$(3 + \varepsilon)^2 = 10$$

for some value ε to be determined. Squaring gives me

$$9 + 2 \cdot 3 \cdot \varepsilon + \varepsilon^2 = 10$$

or

$$2 \cdot 3 \cdot \varepsilon + \varepsilon^2 = 10 - 9$$

$$2 \cdot (3 \cdot \varepsilon) + \varepsilon^2 = 1 \qquad\qquad (C)$$

Now my problem is that of finding ε (which, I note, is less than 1). Because I wish to do this approximation in decimal fractions, I'll write that

$$\varepsilon = \frac{e}{10} + \varepsilon_1$$

where e is some whole number, and ε_1 is the fraction left over. Substituting this into (C) gives me

$$2 \cdot 3 \left(\frac{e}{10} + \varepsilon_1\right) + \left(\frac{e}{10} + \varepsilon_1\right)^2 = 1$$

or

$$2 \cdot 3 \frac{e}{10} + \left(\frac{e}{10}\right)^2 + 2 \cdot 3\varepsilon_1 + 2\varepsilon_1 \frac{e}{10} + \varepsilon_1^2 = 1$$

so

$$2 \cdot 3\varepsilon_1 + 2\varepsilon_1 \frac{e}{10} + \varepsilon_1^2 = 1 - \frac{e}{10}\left(2 \cdot 3 + \frac{e}{10}\right)$$

Now I choose e as large as possible so that the righthand side of this equation is positive. That is, $e = 1$ and hence

$$2 \cdot 3\varepsilon_1 + 2\varepsilon_1 \frac{e}{10} + \varepsilon_1^2 = 1 - .1(6.1)$$

$$= .39$$

or

$$2\left(3 + \frac{e}{10}\right)\varepsilon_1 + \varepsilon_1^2 = .39$$

$$2(3.1 \cdot \varepsilon_1) + \varepsilon_1^2 = .39 \qquad\qquad (D)$$

Note that the format of (D) is quite similar to (C) in that, on the lefthand side, (C) differs from (D) primarily with respect to the order of the

---

[10] This, although streamlined a bit, was still a staple in the high school algebra texts of the 1950s.

approximation—that is, 3.1 and 3, respectively. Making use of this pattern, I continue as before, choosing my hundredths digit e_1 such that

$$.39 - \frac{e_1}{100}\left(2 \cdot (3.1) + \frac{e_1}{100}\right) \tag{E}$$

is the smallest positive number possible. That is, $e_1 = 6$ and my new approximation to $\sqrt{10}$ is 3.16. This process can be continued. I double the previous estimate a—in the above, 3.1—and choose my next decimal digit d—in the above, .06—so that the product $d(2a + d)$—in the above, .06(6.2 + .06)—reduces the righthand side—in the above, .39—as much as positively possible.[11]

P R O B L E M   9 . 3

Determine $\sqrt{10}$ (a) to the thousandths digit and (b) to the ten-thousandths digit.

There are tables for the square roots, just as in Babylonian times. The square root of 2 and the square roots of some other positive integers are known to more than ten million digits. I note that the cube root of 2 can be manually computed by utilizing the expansion of $(a + b)^3$ in a manner similar to that for the square root.

✹ The Reals from a Developmental Perspective

Both $\sqrt{2}$ and π are present in the upper-level elementary mathematics curriculum. Students are engaged in activities where they compute π by measuring—perhaps as the Babylonians did—the circumference of various circular objects and determining the ratio of circumference to diameter. There are also activities that bear some similarity to the methodology employed by Archimedes, although students measure the sides of the inscribed and circumscribed regular polygons.[12] These activities quite often lead into discussion of the data accumulated in such measurements.

Discussion of $\sqrt{2}$, on the other hand, seems to arise when the notion of square root is first introduced and may come up in discussions of the Pythagorean theorem. Students, not surprisingly, find it puzzling that you can draw a square with unit sides but cannot accurately measure the diagonal. However, perhaps because circle measurement is more of a mainstay of the elementary curriculum than diagonal measurement, treatment of such irrational distances is seldom taken up.

In either case there seems to be little discussion in the elementary mathematics classroom of how such approximations might be arithmetically combined and how errors due to approximation might affect totals or products.[13]

---

[11] There is actually little need for decimal arithmetic, as you can see if you multiply (E) by 100. In fact, the usual implementation of this algorithm eliminates writing the decimal point in a manner reminiscent of long division.
[12] These activities usually involve regular polygons with well below ten sides.
[13] There does, however, seem to be some concern with such matters in the elementary science classroom.

Nonetheless, as somewhat of a "thought experiment," consider the following vignette (which should sound somewhat familiar).

> Mr. Batista's sixth grade class has been working with decimal approximations to various measurements. Although his class has discussed how to represent such approximations, they have not discussed how to add them. As an introductory lesson, he has designed the following problem:
>
> > Pretend you are a jeweler. Sometimes people come in to get rings resized. When you cut down a ring to make it smaller, you keep the small portion of gold in exchange for the work you have done. Recently you have collected these amounts:
> >
> > 1.14 grams, .089 gram, and .3 gram
> >
> > You used a scale accurate to within .01 of a gram to determine the 1.14 grams, a scale accurate to within .1 of a gram to determine the .3 gram, and a scale accurate to within .001 gram to determine the .089 gram. Now you have a repair job to do for which you need some gold. You are wondering whether you have enough. Work together with your group to figure out approximately how much gold you have collected. Be prepared to show the class your solution.
>
> Mr. Batista circulates among the working students. He stops to listen to Jeanine, Paul, and Steve. Jeanine looks up and says, "I think we did something like this in Ms. Stowe's class last year." Paul adds, "Yeah, all we have to do is line up the decimals and add." Mr. Batista replies, "Yes, it is like that problem. However, it is also different. What's the difference?" Steve says quietly, "I think it has something to do with the scales."
>
> After the groups finished their work, the class as a whole had a discussion. Eric reported that the students in his group thought that there might be as much as 1.584 grams and as little as 1.475 grams. Paul immediately asked Eric, "Why those numbers?" because if you lined up the numbers and added, you got 1.529 grams. Eric responded that, for instance, since you could measure the .3 gram only to within .1 of a gram, then its actual weight could be anywhere between .25 gram and .35 gram.

✖ Arithmetic with the Reals

It is tempting to suppose that a way out of the difficulties faced by Mr. Batista's class is to make all the weighings on a single very accurate scale. A moment of reflection, however, should convince you that certain difficulties still remain. Real measurements are inherently inaccurate (which doesn't mean that they cannot be made more accurately).

Taking a deeper look at what is going on, let's explore a somewhat analogous problem: the adding of $.\overline{2} + .\overline{3}$. Because both of these numbers are nonterminating decimals, I cannot represent them—within a base-10 place value system—exactly. I can, however, express them as a terminating decimal to various degrees of accuracy.[14] This approach, essentially formalized in the early 1900s, enables me, in spite of there being no *first* right-hand digit in a nonterminating decimal expansion, to apply—with some care—my knowledge of arithmetic to the rationals.[15] The answer to $.\overline{2} + .\overline{3}$ being the ever more accurate result of that operation given the ever more accurate representation of $.\overline{2}$ and $.\overline{3}$.

For example,

$$.\overline{2} = .222222222222 + .0000000000002$$
$$.\overline{3} = .333333333333 + .0000000000003$$

or

$$.\overline{2} = .222222222222 + \varepsilon_1$$
$$.\overline{3} = .333333333333 + \varepsilon_2$$

where $0 < \varepsilon_1, \varepsilon_2 < 10^{-12}$. Thus

$$.\overline{2} + .\overline{3} = .222222222222 + \varepsilon_1 + .333333333333 + \varepsilon_2$$
$$= .555555555555 + \varepsilon_1 + \varepsilon_2$$

where $0 < \varepsilon_1 + \varepsilon_2 < 2 \cdot 10^{-12}$, and we say that

$$.\overline{2} + .\overline{3} = .555555555555$$

with an error of, at most, $2 \cdot 10^{-12}$. In fact, because I could adopt successively more accurate approximations to $.\overline{2}$ and $.\overline{3}$, I could say that

$$.\overline{2} + .\overline{3} = .\overline{5}$$

with an infinitely small error—that is, in the limit of my approximations.

P R O B L E M   9 . 4

In a similar manner, add $.\overline{3}$ and $.\overline{142857}$ (that is, $\frac{1}{3}$ and $\frac{1}{7}$) and check your calculations by adding the respective fractions and writing the decimal expansion for that total.

A similar argument works for subtraction, although I need to be careful about how I compute the error term. Consider $\frac{1}{7} - \frac{1}{9}$:

$$.\overline{142857} - .\overline{1}$$

I have

$$.\overline{142857} = .142857142857142857 + \varepsilon_1$$
$$.\overline{1} = .111111111111111111 + \varepsilon_2$$

---

[14] I am using roughly the notion of what is termed a *Cauchy sequence* here. From this viewpoint a real number is, in a sense, the limit of ever-more-accurate approximations.
[15] Note that if I did not implement such a technique, I would need to jettison the power of the standard addition algorithm.

where $0 < \varepsilon_1, \varepsilon_2 < 10^{-12}$. Thus

$$\overline{.142857} - .\overline{1} = .031746031746031746 + \varepsilon_1 - \varepsilon_2$$

because $-10^{-13} < \varepsilon_1 - \varepsilon_2 < 10^{-12}$. So

$$\overline{.142857} - .\overline{1} = .031746031746031746$$

with an error of, at most, $\pm 10^{-12}$. In fact, because I could adopt successively more accurate approximations to $.\overline{142857}$ and $.\overline{1}$, I could say that, with infinitely small error,

$$\overline{.142857} - .\overline{1} = .\overline{031746}$$

P R O B L E M   9 . 5

Check this result by subtracting the respective fractions and writing a decimal expansion of the difference.

Note that when real numbers that vary in their precision (that is, in the magnitude of their error terms) are added or subtracted, the error in the sum or difference is roughly of the same magnitude as the error in the last precise term. As a case in point, I represent $.\overline{2}$ and $.\overline{3}$, respectively, by

$$.\overline{2} = .222 + .000\overline{2}$$
$$.\overline{3} = .333333333333 + .000000000000\overline{3}$$

or

$$.\overline{2} = .222 + \varepsilon_1$$
$$.\overline{3} = .333333333333 + \varepsilon_2$$

where $0 < \varepsilon_1 < 10^{-3}; 0 < \varepsilon_2 < 10^{-12}$. I have

$$.\overline{2} + .\overline{3} = .222 + \varepsilon_1 + .333333333333 + \varepsilon_2$$
$$= .555333333333 + \varepsilon_1 + \varepsilon_2$$

where $0 < \varepsilon_1 + \varepsilon_2 < 10^{-3} (1 + 10^{-9})$. Thus, that extra precision in my representation of $.\overline{3}$ adds little to the precision in my total. In fact, the best I can say (note that I add only the digits in the least accurate quantity) is that

$$.\overline{2} + .\overline{3} = .555$$

with an error of, at most, $10^3 (1 + 10^{-9}) \approx 10^2$.

P R O B L E M   9 . 6

Why might Eric of Mr. Batista's class argue that an answer to the gold-weighing problem was 1.5 grams accurate to .1 gram?

Multiplication of real numbers is reasonably straightforward, although it does present an intriguing twist. Consider $3 \cdot .\overline{3}$. Writing

$$.\overline{3} = .333333333333 + \varepsilon$$

where $0 < \varepsilon < 10^{-12}$, I have

$$3 \cdot .\overline{3} = .999999999999 + 3\varepsilon$$

where $0 < 3\varepsilon < 3 \cdot 10^{-12}$. Thus, as I can estimate $.\overline{3}$ ever more accurately:

$$3 \cdot .\overline{3} = .\overline{9}$$

On the other hand, we know that $3 \cdot \frac{1}{3} - 1$, and 1 doesn't look like $.\overline{9}$. However, note that

$$1 = .999999999999 + .000000000001$$
$$= .999999999999 + \varepsilon$$

where $0 < \varepsilon < 10^{-12}$. Thus, given how I have framed the arithmetic of reals,

$$1 = .\overline{9}$$

because 1 is the limit of $.\overline{9}$. That is, the real numbers 1 and $.\overline{9}$ are, in effect, identical.

P R O B L E M   9 . 7

Compute $\overline{3} \cdot .\overline{6}$. [*Hint:* First multiply single digits, double digits, and so on until you see the pattern.]

⚔ Pythagorean Theorem

The Pythagorean Theorem is one of the more celebrated theorems in history and was apparently known to the Babylonians as early as 1000 BC. It states that in a right triangle,

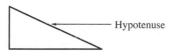

the sum of the squares of the two sides is equal to the square of the hypotenuse. For example, if the lengths of the sides are 3 inches and 4 inches, respectively, then the length of the hypotenuse is 5 inches. There are, it seems, over 300 proofs of this theorem. One was even devised by a U.S. president, James Garfield.

I'll sketch one of the more visually appealing proofs. I construct a triangle

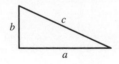

and three copies and rearrange them as follows:

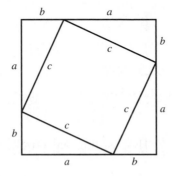

The area of each triangle is $\frac{ab}{2}$. The area of the outer square is $(a + b)^2$, and the area of the inner square is c^2. Thus

$$(a + b)^2 = 4 \cdot \frac{ab}{2} + c^2$$

or

$$a^2 + 2ab + b^2 = 2ab + c^2$$

so

$$a^2 + b^2 = c^2 \tag{F}$$

as was to be shown.

As I have noted, a solution to (F) is the triple 3, 4, 5. An interesting mathematical question is whether there are any more whole-number solutions. I will sketch a method to find all such solutions of (F) that have no pairwise common factor.[16] That is, it is not the case: that a and b have a common factor, that a and c have a common factor, or that b and c have a common factor.

> *Case 1:* Assume that a and b are both odd. That is, $a = 2n + 1$ and $b = 2m + 1$. In that case c^2, and hence c, must be even. That is, $c = 2s$. Substituting this value for c in (F) gives
>
> $$(2n + 1)^2 + (2m + 1)^2 = (2s)^2$$

---

[16] Note that this is equivalent to a, b, and c having no common factor.

or

$$4n^2 + 4n + 1 + 4m^2 + 4m + 1 = 4s^2$$

so

$$4n^2 + 4m^2 + 4n + 4m + 2 = 4s^2$$

or

$$4(n^2 + m^2) + 4(n + m) + 2 = 4s^2$$

However, this is impossible, so *a and b cannot both be odd.*

P R O B L E M   9 . 8

Why is $4(n^2 + m^2) + 4(n + m) + 2 = 4s^2$ impossible?

Case 2: I assume that *a* is even and *b* is odd. Thus *c* and *b* must be odd.

P R O B L E M   9 . 9

Why must *c* and *b* both be odd?

And I write (F) as

$$a^2 = c^2 - b^2$$

or, factoring,

$$a^2 = (c - b)(c + b)$$

Thus

$$\left(\frac{a}{2}\right)^2 = \left(\frac{c + b}{2}\right)\left(\frac{c - b}{2}\right) \tag{G}$$

Note that a, $c - b$, and $c + b$ are even.

P R O B L E M   9 . 1 0

Why is $c - b$ even?

Now

$$\frac{c + b}{2} + \frac{c - b}{2} = c$$

$$\frac{c + b}{2} - \frac{c - b}{2} = b$$

so if some number d is a common factor of $\frac{c+b}{2}$ and $\frac{c-b}{2}$, then d must be a common factor of b and c. This, according to my initial assumptions, is impossible.

This means that because the left-hand side of (G) is a square, both $\frac{c+b}{2}$ and $\frac{c-b}{2}$ must be squares. Let's think together about this step

Remember the Fundamental Theorem of Arithmetic: Every composite number N can be factored uniquely into prime factors:

$$N = p_1^{a_1}p_2^{a_2}\cdots p_r^{a_r}$$

where the p_i's are the various different prime factors and a_i's are the multiplicities—that is, the number of times p_i occurs in the prime factorization.

Thus $\frac{a}{2}$ is of the form

$$\frac{a}{2} = p_1^{a_1}p_2^{a_2}\cdots p_r^{a_r}$$

and hence,

$$\left(\frac{a}{2}\right)^2 = (p_1^{a_1})^2(p_2^{a_2})^2\cdots(p_r^{a_r})^2$$

or

$$\left(\frac{c+b}{2}\right)\left(\frac{c-b}{2}\right) = (p_1^{a_1})^2(p_2^{a_2})^2\cdots(p_r^{a_r})^2$$

Now, for example, if p_1 divides $\frac{c+b}{2}$, then $(p_1^{a_1})^2$ must divide $\frac{c+b}{2}$.

P R O B L E M   9 . 1 1

Why, if p_1 divides $\frac{c+b}{2}$, must $(p_1^{a_1})^2$ divide $\frac{c+b}{2}$?

And thus, for example, $\frac{c+b}{2}$ must be of the form

$$\frac{c+b}{2} = (q_1^{b_1})^2(q_2^{b_2})^2\cdots(q_s^{b_s})^2$$

where the q_i's are primes and the b_i's are their respective multiplicities. Thus, I write

$$\frac{c+b}{2} = u^2$$

$$\frac{c-b}{2} = v^2$$

and, substituting this into (G), I have

$$a = 2uv$$
$$b = u^2 - v^2$$
$$c = u^2 + v^2$$

Note that u and v can be any two whole numbers such that $u > v$; that u and v have no factors other than 1 in common; and that u and v cannot both be odd. For example, for $u = 2$ and $v = 1$, I have $a = 4$, $b = 3$, and $c = 5$.

P R O B L E M   9 . 1 2

Using these formulas for a, b, and c, find two more whole-number solutions for (F). Find a triplet of fractions j, k, p that satisfy (F).

✼ Continued Fractions

I have shown $\sqrt{2}$ is irrational and hence has a nonterminating, nonrepeating decimal expansion. But this does not mean that we cannot represent $\sqrt{2}$ in a systematic fashion. For instance, I know that $1 < \sqrt{2} < 2$, so I set

$$x = 1 + \sqrt{2} \tag{H}$$

Rearranging gives me

$$x - 1 = \sqrt{2}$$

and squaring both sides yields

$$(x - 1)(x - 1) = x^2 - 2 \cdot x + 1$$
$$= 2$$

or

$$x^2 = 2 \cdot x + 1$$

Dividing through by x (x is clearly non-zero) on both sides gives

$$x = 2 + \frac{1}{x} \tag{I}$$

Substituting (I) in (H) gives

$$1 + \sqrt{2} = 2 + \frac{1}{x}$$

or

$$\sqrt{2} = 1 + \frac{1}{x} \tag{J}$$

and repeatedly substituting for (I) in (J) gives

$$\sqrt{2} = 1 + \cfrac{1}{2 + \cfrac{1}{2 + \cfrac{1}{2 + \cdots}}}$$

Such expansions are termed *continued fraction expansions*. Two among the others we know are

$$\text{The Golden Ratio} = 1 + \cfrac{1}{1 + \cfrac{1}{1 + \cfrac{1}{1 + \cdots}}}$$

and

$$\frac{4}{\pi} = 1 + \cfrac{1^2}{2 + \cfrac{3^2}{2 + \cfrac{5^2}{2 + \cfrac{7^2}{2 + \cdots}}}}$$

P R O B L E M   9 . 1 3

Give a continued fraction expansion for $\sqrt{7}$.

Investigations

1. One modern version of the square root algorithm reads as follows: Write the original number in decimal form with a line above; the root will be written on this line. Now separate the digits into pairs, starting from the decimal point and going both left and right; you may need to add leading and trailing zeros to pad out the beginning and ending pairs. The decimal point of the root will be above the decimal point of the square. One digit of the root will appear above each pair of digits of the square.

   Beginning with the leftmost pair of digits, do the following procedure for each pair:

   a. Starting on the left, bring down the most significant (leftmost) pair of digits not yet used (if all the digits have been used, write "00") and write them to the right of the remainder from the previous step (on the first step, there will be no remainder). That is, in effect, multiply the remainder by 100 and add the two digits. I'll denote this value by C.

   b. Let R denote the root, ignoring the decimal point, that has been determined so far (on the first step, $R = 0$). Determine the greatest digit d such that

   $$C \geq d \cdot (20 \cdot R + d)$$

   Note that on the first step, this is equivalent to finding d such that $C \geq d^2$.

c. The digit d is the next digit in the root, so place it in the appropriate location on the line above the square and subtract:

$$C - d \cdot (20 \cdot R + d)$$

d. If this remainder is zero and there are no more digit pairs to bring down, then you have finished. Otherwise, set C equal to the remainder, go back to step a, and continue.

Prove that this algorithm, like my adaptation of Theon's algorithm, approximates the taking of the square to, in theory, any required accuracy. *Hint:* Compare the steps in my adaptation of Theon's algorithm for taking the square root of 10 to the steps in this algorithm:

```
    3.1  6  2  2
  10.00 00 00 00
   1 00              1 · (20 · 3 + 1) = 61
    61
   39 00             6 · (20 · (31) + 6) = 3,756
   37 56
    1 44 00          2 · (20 · (316) + 2) = 12,644
    1 26 44
      17 56 00       2 · (20 · (3162) + 2) = 126,484
      12 64 84
       4 91 16
```

2. In a previous section of this chapter, I illustrated a method for giving nonzero, pairwise prime, integer solutions to

$$a^2 + b^2 = c^2$$

An obvious question is what to do about

$$a^3 + b^3 = c^3$$

or

$$a^n + b^n = c^n$$

where $3 < n$.

   In 1637 Pierre de Fermat wrote, in his copy of Claude-Gaspar Bachet's translation of Diophantus' *Arithmetica*, "However, it is impossible to write a cube as the sum of two cubes, a fourth power as the sum of two fourth powers, and in general any power beyond the second as the sum of two similar powers. For this I have discovered a truly marvelous proof, but the margin is too small to contain it."[17] No correct proof of this conjecture—which is termed Fermat's Last Theorem—was found for 357 years until one was given, in 1995, by Andrew Wiles. Sketch the history of Fermat's Last Theorem.

---

[17] Oystein Ore, *Number Theory and Its History* (New York: McGraw-Hill, 1948), p. 204.

3. In mathematics and the arts, two quantities are in the *Golden Ratio* if the ratio between the sum of those quantities and the larger quantity is the same as the ratio between the larger quantity and the smaller quantity. As early as the Renaissance, believing this proportion to be aesthetically pleasing, artists proportioned their works to approximate the Golden Ratio—especially in the form of the golden rectangle, in which the ratio of the longer side to the shorter is the Golden Ratio.

    Prove that the golden ratio, φ, is given by

$$\varphi = \frac{1 + \sqrt{5}}{2}$$

4. Give an example of a rule for writing the decimal digits of an irrational number, and prove that the number that is generated must be irrational. [*Hint:* Remember that all nonterminating repeating decimal expansions are rational.]

CHAPTER 10

Transfinite Numbers

The term *infinite* has come up a number of times in this book, and I have treated it more or less informally. But in this chapter you and I are going to explore the art and practice of *transfinite* arithmetic. This is a somewhat peculiar topic, because infinite numbers aren't numbers in a sense in which we usually think of. Nonetheless, with some help from five-year-old Peter whom we met in Chapter 2, I can talk about the usual arithmetic operations.

Let's begin with some history, because the idea of the infinite has always captivated and puzzled. Then we'll take a look into the classroom to see how the infinite, so to speak, enters into the doings and thinking of children. This will prepare the way for a discussion of some different varieties of infinity, and some rather arcane arithmetic. For instance,

$$\aleph_0 + 2008 = \aleph_0$$
$$\aleph_0 - 2008 = \aleph_0$$
$$2008 \cdot \aleph_0 = \aleph_0$$
$$\aleph_0 \div 2008 = \aleph_0$$

where $\aleph_0$ is the cardinality of the set of all counting numbers.

ℵ Infinity from a Historical Perspective

The possibility of very large numbers has fascinated children and mathematicians throughout the ages. Vedic mathematicians writing around the fifth century BC had individual Sanskrit names for certain of the powers of 10. For instance,

koti	10^7
samaptalambha	10^{39}
nirabbuda	10^{63}
dhvajagranishamani	10^{421}

Much like these early Vedic mathematicians, the Jains (a religious sect in India) had an interest in the enumeration of very large numbers. This interest led, around 400 BC, to a classification of numbers into three groups and three orders within those groups:[1]

[1] George Gheverghese Joseph, *The Crest of the Peacock: Non-European Roots of Mathematics* (New York: Penguin, 1991), p. 250.

1.   Enumerable numbers: lowest, intermediate, highest
2.   Innumerable numbers: nearly innumerable, truly innumerable, and innumerably innumerable
3.   Infinite numbers: nearly infinite, truly infinite, and infinitely infinite

The highest enumerable number of the Jains corresponds to the cardinality of the counting numbers $\aleph_0$.

The Greeks, on the other hand, viewed talk of the infinite with some suspicion. They designated the infinite as *apeiron,* something unbounded, indefinite, or undefined; as the absence (so to speak) of limit and, in a sense, on the verge of chaos. The infinite also was a component in the paradoxes of Zeno, the best known of which is that of Achilles and the Hare (or, as it has become known, the Hare and the Tortoise):

> A hare is chasing a tortoise. The tortoise starts some distance ahead—let's say 10 yards. They both start running at the same time. The hare runs at a speed of 10 yards every second, and the tortoise runs at a speed of 1 yard every second. After 1 second the hare has reached the tortoise's starting position, but the tortoise has moved 1 yard in that same time, so the hare has not caught up yet. The tortoise is now 1 yard ahead, but by the time the hare travels 1 yard, the tortoise has traveled $\frac{1}{10}$ of a yard. That is, the tortoise is now $\frac{1}{10}$ of a yard ahead, but by the time the hare travels $\frac{1}{10}$ of a yard, the tortoise has traveled $\frac{1}{100}$ of a yard. The tortoise is now $\frac{1}{100}$ of a yard ahead.

I could keep going on indefinitely, but the tortoise is always a bit farther ahead when the hare gets to where the tortoise was.

P R O B L E M   1 0 . 1

Is Zeno correct in saying the hare never catches the tortoise? If so, why? If not, why not?

Aristotle, perhaps in part because of the paradoxes of Zeno, argued in his *Physics* that

> Since no sensible magnitude is infinite, it is impossible to exceed every assigned magnitude; for if it were possible there would be something bigger than the heavens.

Thus the counting numbers, having no greatest number, were labeled by Aristotle as *potentially infinite.* Such a stance toward the infinite seems to have been quite influential in Western mathematics. For example, Karl Friedrich Gauss, a prominent mathematician writing in the 1800s, admonishes a colleague, saying, "As to your proof, I must protest most vehemently against your use of the infinite as something consummated, as this is never permitted in mathematics. The infinite is but a figure of speech. . . ."

Infinity was given its mathematical footing in Western mathematics by Georg Cantor in 1874. His results, some of which I will discuss in a moment, unleashed a storm of controversy. He was condemned by a number of the more influential mathematicians of his time. And this condemnation, though ultimately shown to be unjustified, adversely affected his mental health.

✖ Infinity from a Developmental Perspective

Infinity enters the elementary mathematics class in the primary grades. As students, in their counting, move from 2 to 5 and on to 10 and 20, there dawns a growing realization that the counting numbers—the natural numbers—never end. This is confirmed in later talk of hundreds, thousands, and even *zillions*. This in itself causes no great consternation. In fact, children of this age are captivated by large numbers. What *does* cause these students consternation is that they are no longer able to verify certain mathematical statements—for example, that an even number plus an odd number is always an odd number—by trying out all combinations of numbers. Consider the following vignette:[2]

> Ms. Ball's third graders have generated a series of conjectures about even and odd numbers. Betsy, illustrating her answer by the addition of 7 + 7, says, "If an odd number plus an odd number, if you add another number with an odd number, then it equals an even number because *an even number plus 1 equals an odd number, so if you added two odd numbers together, you can add the 1's left over and it would always equal an even number.*"

> During subsequent class discussion, Mei voices her concern about whether this is always true. She says, "I don't think so, because you don't know the numbers, like, you don't even know how you pronounce it, or how you say it . . . . I don't think it would work for numbers we can't say or figure out what they are."

Although Mei is correct in her characterization of numbers (remember the *mega* of Chapter 2), Betsy has supplied the beginning of a quite acceptable deductive proof. Infinity, in situations such as this, can provide substantial motivation for proofs beyond those of simple exhaustion, as this continuation indicates:

> Some time later, Ms. Ball's students report on their work on even and odd numbers. Mark reports on his work with Nathan: "Well, first, me and Nathan, we were just getting answers and we weren't thinking about proof. And we were still getting answers and [then] we were trying to prove, and Betsy came and she had proved it, and then we all agreed that it would work."

---

[2] Adapted from Deborah Loewenberg Ball and Hyman Bass, Making mathematics reasonable in school. In *A Research Companion to Principles and Standards for School Mathematics*, ed. J. Kilpatrick, W. G. Martin, and D. Shifter (Reston, VA: NCTM, 2003).

Infinity also can enter the classroom via solutions to various problems. Consider the following vignette.

Ms. Lukas has posed the following problem to her third grade class:

> You have four cookies that you wish to divide equally among two friends and yourself. How much cookie do you and each of your friends get?

Ms. Lukas walks around the class as her students are working. She stops to talk to Vanessa. Vanessa shows her the picture she has drawn.

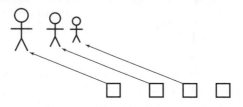

Ms. Lukas, somewhat puzzled, asks Vanessa about the unallocated cookie. Vanessa takes the paper back, adds some lines, and again hands it to Ms. Lukas, saying, "They each get one and one-fourth."

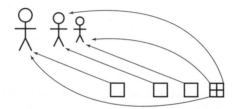

Ms. Lukas says, "But you still have a piece left over." Yvonne replies, "Oh, you can divide that up into fourths also and just keep on going forever. What do you call those little pieces, anyway?" Ms. Lukas, somewhat bemused, replies, "A fourth of a fourth." Yvonne smiles and says, "They now each get one and one-fourth of a cookie plus one-fourth of one-fourth."

Yvonne has just provided a nice demonstration that $\frac{4}{3}$ can be represented by the infinite series[3]

$$1 + \frac{1}{4} + \frac{1}{4} \cdot \frac{1}{4} + \frac{1}{4} \cdot \frac{1}{4} \cdot \frac{1}{4} + \cdots$$

or

$$\frac{4}{3} = 1 + \sum_{n=1}^{\infty} \left(\frac{1}{4}\right)^n$$

P R O B L E M   1 0 . 2

Write an *infinite* series for $\frac{1}{3}$ in terms of powers of $\frac{1}{4}$.

---

[3] Note that while Yvonne realizes that she can continue to subdivide (although it gets harder to do so as the pieces get smaller) and realizes that she continues to add the bits onto each person's share, she is not thinking of this as an infinite series representation of $\frac{4}{3}$.

P R O B L E M   1 0 . 3

Write an infinite series for $\frac{1}{7}$ in terms of powers of $\frac{1}{8}$. [*Hint:* Note this is equivalent to the cookie problem of dividing 8 cookies among seven people.]

✦ Varieties of Infinity

What is important in Yvonne's approach to the cookie problem is her step-by-step use of the natural numbers. Her first division allocates one cookie to a person; her second division allocates another fourth to each person; her third a sixteenth; and so on. Infinity for Yvonne becomes, in practice, the totality of the counting numbers. This is similar, as I have indicated, to where Cantor began.

Let me take a deeper look with five-year-old Peter as my guide. Remember that Peter was faced with the task of counting the set C of seven candies:

Tagging the first *one* and successively incrementally tagging each until he reaches the last and seventh, Peter is able to tell his teacher, Ms. Jannat, that the cardinality—how many there are in the set—is 7. If you think about it, Peter could, in principle, do this with any set of objects. He might run out of names for the numbers (as Mei suggested), but with some help in that regard, he could certainly tag each one and pronounce the cardinality. In fact, Peter could count up toward a mega. Counting to a mega isn't practically possible, and there might be a lot of new number names along the way (as suggested by the Vedic mathematicians), but in principle, it could be done.

Now, you need to make a big conceptual leap. You are able to imagine Peter counting to 7 and even to 100. You can imagine him counting, with help, to 1000, and in principle, you should be able to imagine him beginning the count to a mega. I want you to imagine him attempting to count all the counting numbers. I suspect that if I asked Peter to do this, he would say, "Simple! I count one as one, two as two, and so on.[4] And if and when I get to the end, that is how many there are." Peter doesn't have a name for how many there are, but Cantor did. He called it aleph-null and wrote it $\aleph_0$.

---

[4] An important point in my story is that Peter isn't just saying the number names as in some sort of chant; rather, he is using the counting numbers to tag each of the candies.

Now some intriguing things happen. Let me do some counting. I'll count the even numbers:

Even Number	Count
2	1
4	2
6	3
⋮	⋮
$2n$	n
⋮	⋮

That is, I have a one-to-one function f associating any even number n with a counting number

$$f(n) = \frac{n}{2}$$

How many even numbers are there? According to the way I've defined *how many*—that is, in terms of cardinality—there are $\aleph_0$, because I have assigned 1 counting number to each even number. So there are *just as many* even numbers as there are counting numbers. This is somewhat strange as given that, of course, the counting numbers include the even numbers.

P R O B L E M   1 0 . 4

Show that there are $\aleph_0$ odd numbers.

How about the integers? Surely there are more integers than counting numbers. Let me try to count them (I'll double-count zero to make a nice pattern).

Integer	Count
-0	1
$+0$	2
-1	3
$+1$	4
⋮	⋮
$-n$	$2n + 1$
$+n$	$2n + 2$
⋮	⋮

so my counting function is

$$f(n) = \begin{cases} 2n + 2 & \text{for } n \text{ positive} \\ \\ -2n + 1 & \text{for } n \text{ negative} \end{cases}$$

Hence, as you can see, there are $\aleph_0$ integers.

Write a function (it may need to have two parts, as above) that doesn't double-count zero. [*Hint:* This may mean you need to count zero as 1 and then proceed as above, counting, perhaps, $+1$ as 2, and -1 as 3, and so on.]

I've shown that the number of integers on the number line

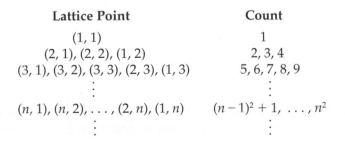

is $\aleph_0$. How about the number of lattice points in the plane? I'll begin to count the positive ones.[5]

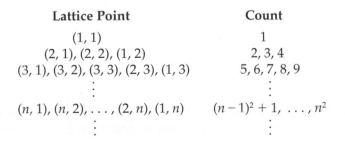

My counting function looks a little more complicated:

Lattice Point	Count
$(1, 1)$	1
$(2, 1), (2, 2), (1, 2)$	$2, 3, 4$
$(3, 1), (3, 2), (3, 3), (2, 3), (1, 3)$	$5, 6, 7, 8, 9$
$\vdots$	$\vdots$
$(n, 1), (n, 2), \ldots, (2, n), (1, n)$	$(n-1)^2 + 1, \ldots, n^2$
$\vdots$	$\vdots$

---

[5] Note that 1 counts the lattice point $(1, 1)$, 2 counts the lattice point $(2, 1)$, 3 counts the lattice point $(2, 2)$, 4 counts the lattice point $(1, 2)$, and so on.

P   R   O   B   L   E   M   1 0 . 6

Demonstrate a method for counting all the lattice points in the plane. (That is, include the lattice points below and to the left of those shown in the diagram.)

Certainly the cardinality of the rational numbers must be larger than the counting numbers. There are, after all, an infinite number of fractions just between 0 and 1 on the number line. Nonetheless, I can count the positive rationals as follows:[6]

Rational	Count
$\frac{1}{1}$	1
$\frac{1}{2}$	2
$\frac{2}{2}$	3
$\frac{2}{1}$	4
$\frac{1}{3}$	5
$\frac{2}{3}$	6
$\frac{3}{3}$	7
$\frac{3}{2}$	8
$\frac{3}{1}$	9
$\vdots$	$\vdots$
$\frac{1}{n}$	$(n-1)^2 + 1$
$\frac{2}{n}$	$(n-1)^2 + 2$
$\vdots$	$\vdots$
$\frac{n}{1}$	n^2
$\vdots$	$\vdots$

How did I come up with all this? Consider a fraction $\frac{a}{b}$. I can represent this by the lattice point (b, a), and I just showed you how to count the positive lattice points.

---

[6] This is a version of Cantor's argument.

P R O B L E M   1 0 . 7

Demonstrate a method for counting all the rationals—positive and negative.

So is $\aleph_0$ all there is? Happily, that is not the case, because I cannot use the counting numbers to count the reals. I'll sketch a version of Cantor's argument.

I'll do a proof by contradiction. Assume I do have such a counting of the reals (remember that I can represent the reals as nonterminating decimal fractions). I'll restrict myself to reals between 0 and 1:

Reals	**Reals**
$.a_1a_2a_3a_4a_5\ldots$	$1\ldots$
$.b_1b_2b_3b_4b_5\ldots$	$2\ldots$
$\vdots$	$\vdots$
$.u_1u_2u_3u_4u_5$	n
$\vdots$	$\vdots$

I'll now create a new number $.v_1v_2v_3v_4v_5\ldots$ such that

$$v_1 \neq a_1$$
$$v_2 \neq b_2$$
$$\vdots$$
$$v_n \neq u_n$$
$$\vdots$$

Assume that this number is in our list. Perhaps it is the mth such number

$$.w_1w_2w_3w_4w_5\ldots$$

But this can't be the case, because $.v_1v_2v_3v_4v_5\ldots$ differs from $.w_1w_2w_3w_4w_5\ldots$ at the mth place. Thus I have a contradiction, so I cannot count the reals with the counting numbers.

I'll represent the cardinality of the reals by c. This transfinite number is also called the cardinality of the continuum or the power of the continuum. It is an open question whether there are any sets with cardinality between c and $\aleph_0$. However, I can show that $c = 10^{\aleph_0}$ as follows:

Remember when, in Chapter 2, I wondered how many different ways Peter might count the candies. I'm going to do something like that here

(I'll consider only the reals between 0 and 1). Any real number between 0 and 1 has the decimal expansion (perhaps terminating)

$$.a_1a_2a_3a_4a_5 \ldots$$

I can choose the first digit after the decimal point in 10 different ways (0, 1, 2, 3, 4, 5, 6, 7, 8, 9). I can choose the second digit after the decimal in 10 different ways, and so on. Because there are $\aleph_0$ digits in the decimal expansion, there are $10^{\aleph_0}$ possibilities for a real number between 0 and 1.

P R O B L E M   1 0 . 8

Prove that $c = 2^{\aleph_0}$.

✖ Arithmetic with Infinite Numbers

Just as before, Peter shows us the way in his counting of candies. (You might want to review Chapter 2, especially that portion dealing with sets.)

Addition

I have a set R of r red candies and a set G of $\aleph_0$ green candies. How many do I have in total? Peter would begin with the red candies and count 1, 2, 3, 4, 5. Then, *counting on*, he would begin with the first of the green candies, counting 6, then 7 for the second of the green candies, and so on, the total—that is, the cardinality of $R \cup G$—being $\aleph_0$. Thus

$$\aleph_0 + 5 = \aleph_0$$

P R O B L E M   1 0 . 9

Prove that $\aleph_0 + N = \aleph_0$ for any finite counting number N.

Subtraction

What if I take away those R candies from the set $R \cup G$? It is clear that I have G left, and hence, I suggest that

$$\aleph_0 - N = \aleph_0 \text{ for any finite counting number } N$$

P R O B L E M   1 0 . 1 0

Prove that $\aleph_0 - N = \aleph_0$ for any finite counting number N.

What if the cardinality of R is $\aleph_0$? In this case, the cardinality of $R \cup G - R$ (I'm assuming the elements of R are different from those of G) is $\aleph_0$. On the other hand, the cardinality of $R - R$ is 0. In fact, the cardinality of the difference of two arbitrary sets of cardinality $\aleph_0$— one containing the other—is somewhat ambiguous.

P R O B L E M   1 0 . 1 1

Construct two infinite sets A and B so that the cardinality of $A - B$ is 5. A should contain B so that taking the difference makes arithmetical sense.

Multiplication

Subtraction seems a little chancy for infinite sets. What about multiplication? Let

$$R = \{r_1, r_2, r_3, \ldots\}$$
$$G = \{g_1, g_2, g_3, \ldots\}$$

be two sets of cardinality $\aleph_0$. Then I can count $R \cup G$ as follows:

Count	Object
1	r_1
2	g_1
3	r_2
4	g_2
$\vdots$	$\vdots$
$2n + 1$	r_n
$2n + 2$	g_n
$\vdots$	$\vdots$

That is, I do it just the way I counted the integers. Thus $\aleph_0 + \aleph_0 = \aleph_0$, or

$$2 \cdot \aleph_0 = \aleph_0$$

P R O B L E M   1 0 . 1 2

Show that $N \cdot \aleph_0 = \aleph_0$ for any finite counting number N.

How about $\aleph_0 \cdot \aleph_0$? Remember those lattice points in the plane:

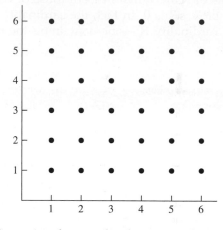

The first row of lattice points has cardinality $\aleph_0$, as does the second and so on. Further, there are $\aleph_0$ rows. Thus $\aleph_0 \cdot \aleph_0 = \aleph_0$.

P R O B L E M   1 0 . 1 3

Show that $\aleph_0{}^N = \aleph_0$ for N a finite counting number [*Hint:* Use induction.]

Division

I'll use the idea of fair sharing to compute such problems as $\aleph_0 \div 3$. For example, assume I have a set C of $\aleph_0$ cookies to divide among three people. Let

$$C = \{c_1, c_2, c_3, c_4, c_5, c_6, c_7, \ldots\}$$

Then

Person 1	**Person 2**	**Person 3**
c_1	c_2	c_3
c_4	c_5	c_6
$\vdots$	$\vdots$	$\vdots$
c_{3n+1}	c_{3n+2}	c_{3n+3}

So each person gets $\aleph_0$ cookies.

P R O B L E M   1 0 . 1 4

Show that $\aleph_0 \div N = \aleph_0$ for any finite counting number N.

What about $\aleph_0 \div \aleph_0$? Because division is related to subtraction, there may be problems. Consider the case when I have $\aleph_0$ people and $\aleph_0$ cookies. I can share them so that each person gets 1. However, I think I could share them so that each person gets two.

P R O B L E M   1 0 . 1 5

How could I share the cookies so that each person got (a) two, (b) three?

Investigations

1. Explore Cantor's mathematical life.
2. In talking about infinity, the mathematician David Hilbert (1862–1943) often told the story of a hotel with $\aleph_0$ rooms. One version of this story goes as follows:[7]

   > A traveler comes to a hotel late at night. He goes to the desk clerk and asks, "How many rooms in this hotel?" The clerk says: "Forty-seven, and every one is occupied." The traveler says: "Can you give me a room?" The clerk says: "No, sorry. Every room is occupied. I already told you."
   >
   > The traveler drives a few more miles, and then comes to the Grand Hotel. He goes to the desk clerk and asks, "How many rooms in this hotel?" The clerk says: "Aleph-Null ($\aleph_0$), and every room is occupied." The traveler says, "Can you give me a room?" The clerk says, "Certainly. I'll just move the tenant of room 1 to room 2 and the tenant in 2 to room 3, and so on. Then you can have room 1."
   >
   > The word gets out and people flock to the Grand Hotel. One day it so happens that $\aleph_0$ people show up. The clerk begins, as usual, to make room by shifting tenants to the next-higher room numbers. However, it becomes clear after the first two new arrivals (and she still has $\aleph_0$ to go), that this is going to take some time. Can you help her out?

   [*Hint:* How about beginning by putting the tenant in room 1 in room 2, putting the tenant in room 2 in room 4, and putting the tenant in room 3 in room 6?]
3. I briefly mentioned the Continuum Hypothesis. Sketch its substance and its history.
4. In the early 1900s a number of mathematicians and philosophers began a (re)examination of the foundations of mathematics to clarify a number of mathematical/philosophical conundrums—Zeno's paradox of the Hare was one among them—once and for all. In this midst of this work (around 1902), Bertrand Russell proposed a *new* paradox that had roughly the following form:

---

[7]As with any good story, adaptations abound. This is one.

You are given a *grouping* of objects R—a member of R might be a single item, a grouping of single items, or a mixture of these possibilities—and from these objects you construct the *grouping* S such that each member P of S is not a member of its own *grouping*. There are, in essence, two cases:

> Case 1: S is not a member of its own *grouping*. However, this implies <u>by definition</u> that S is a member of S, and <u>by assumption</u>, S is not a member of S.
>
> Case 2: S is a member of its own *grouping*. However, this implies <u>by definition</u> that S is not a member of S, and <u>by assumption</u>, S is a member of S.

Perhaps you can suggest a way out of this paradox, but in any case, sketch the response of Russell and the mathematical community of that time.

5. I have confined much of my discussion of the infinite to transfinite cardinal numbers. However, there are also the transfinite ordinal numbers. In a sense Cantor's approach is reasonably straightforward. I begin counting, and when I get past the counting numbers, I'm at ω. The next such number is, of course, $\omega + 1$ and so on.

   Things become quite interesting when I take up addition, because with ordinals, I, in effect, count on. That is, say I start with 5 and wish to add 4 more. I would say, "*Five*, six, seven, eight, nine. I have nine." Using this approach, add (a) 1 plus ω and (b) ω plus 1. Remember to explain your answers.

Appendix
Tools for Understanding

This appendix contains a potpourri of items that I thought would be helpful in reading this text and that seemed best addressed outside that reading. To this end, I have briefly discussed the notion of variables; have clarified some of the notation I employ for subscripts and exponents; have listed some of the important properties of arithmetic (properties that are often taken for granted); and have, because its truth is assumed in several chapters, provided a proof of the Fundamental Theorem of Arithmetic.

Variables

Variables are crucial to any mathematical conversation, and they occur informally very early in children's talk about mathematics. For example, a teacher might ask a child, "What number do you have if you add one to five?" and after the child said, "Six," the teacher might say, "How do you know that?" If the child responds, "If you add one to any number you just get one more," the phrase *any number* is being used as a variable.

Let's look at another example. Suppose you and I are talking about even and odd numbers and I say, "The sum of two odd numbers is always even." You say, "Yeah, three plus three is six and five plus three is eight." I might say, "But I meant the sum of *any* two odd numbers is even." By this I mean that if n represents any odd number and m represents any odd number, then their sum $n + m$ is even. Here n and m are variables, because I haven't specified their value. In your example, n could be 3 and m could be 3 (or n could be 5 and m could be 3).

The power of such language is apparent when we reflect on what an even number is; for example, it is 2 times some number. Think about this a bit. Two, for example, is 2 times 1, and 52 is 2 times 26. Thus, generalizing somewhat, because odd numbers are just 1 plus even numbers, we can say that an odd number is 2 times some number plus 1. Thus, for example, 3 is 2 times 1 plus 1, and 53 is two times 26 plus 1.

Therefore, I might write in variable notation, where N and M now represent *any number*, that any two odd numbers are represented by

$$2 \cdot N + 1$$
$$2 \cdot M + 1$$

What is the sum of these numbers? Rearranging slightly, I have

$$2 \cdot N + 1 + 2 \cdot M + 1 = 2 \cdot N + 2 \cdot M + 2$$

and using the distributive property (which I will talk about in more detail momentarily) gives

$$2 \cdot N + 1 + 2 \cdot M + 1 = 2 \cdot N + 2 \cdot M + 2$$
$$= 2(N + M + 1)$$

However, by definition $2(N + M + 1)$ is an even number, and hence I have proved, in a fairly efficient manner using *variables*, that the sum of any two odd numbers is even.

Subscripts and Exponents

In this text I have used two common shorthand notations without much explanation. The first of these are exponents—for example, 2^3, which is pronounced "two-cubed" or "two to the third power." By this, I mean simply the product

$$2 \cdot 2 \cdot 2 = 8$$

There are some special cases:

$$1^1 = 1$$
$$2^1 = 2$$
$$3^1 = 3$$
$$\vdots$$

[This means "and so on."]

and

$$1^0 = 1$$
$$2^0 = 1$$
$$3^0 = 1$$
$$\vdots$$

The rule for negative exponents is simply that when n is a non-zero number and k is a positive integer, then

$$n^{-k} = \frac{1}{n^k}$$

Note that I take 0^0 to be undefined.

Subscripts provide a handy notation for systematically distinguishing variables. For instance, to symbolically distinguish five apples, I might write

$$a_1, a_2, a_3, a_4, a_5$$

This would be spoken formally as "*a* sub-one, *a* sub-two, *a* sub-three, *a* sub-four, and *a*-sub 5" and a little less formally as "*a* one, *a* two, *a* three, *a* four, *a* five."

Fundamental Properties of Arithmetic

In case you have forgotten, let's review the distributive property and certain of the other fundamental properties of arithmetic. In what follows I will use the variable notation n, m, and p to denote any three real numbers. Note that we, as teachers, assume explicitly or implicitly some knowledge of all of these properties in the elementary mathematics curriculum.

Commutative Property of Addition

$n + m = m + n$ Example: $2 + 3 = 3 + 2$

Associative Property of Addition

$(n + m) + p = n + (m + p)$ Example: $(2 + 3) + 5 = 2 + (3 + 5)$

Commutative Property of Multiplication

$n \cdot m = m \cdot n$ Example: $2 \cdot 3 = 3 \cdot 2$

Associative Property of Multiplication

$(n \cdot m) \cdot p = m \cdot (n \cdot p)$ Example: $(2 \cdot 3) \cdot 5 = 2 \cdot (3 \cdot 5)$

Distributive Property

$n \cdot (m + p) = n \cdot m + n \cdot p$ Example: $2 \cdot (3 + 5) = 2 \cdot 3 + 2 \cdot 5$

Additive Cancellation

If $m + p = n + p$, then $m = n$.   Example: $3 + 5 = 3 + 5$ so $5 = 5$

Multiplicative Cancellation

Let p be non-zero.
If $m \cdot p = n \cdot p$, then $m = n$.   Example: $2 \cdot 3 = 2 \cdot 3$, so $2 = 2$

Total Ordering

For all m, n, either $m \leq n$ or $n \leq m$.

Fundamental Theorem of Arithmetic

The theorem states that every composite number N can be factored uniquely into prime factors:

$$N = p_1^{a_1} p_2^{a_2} \cdots p_r^{a_r} \tag{A}$$

where the p_i's are the various different prime factors and a_i is the multiplicity—that is, the number of times p_i occurs in the prime factorization. The proof I give is largely attributable to Euclid, but Karl Friedrich Gauss offered the first complete proof.

Proof: I need to show that (1) every composite number can be represented as in (A), and (2) this is a unique representation.

Representation. I proceed by contradiction and suppose that there is a positive composite integer—that is, it is neither 1 nor a prime—that cannot be factored as a product of primes. Then, by the well-ordering principle,[1] there must be a smallest such number N. However, because N is composite,

$$N = a \cdot b \qquad\qquad (B)$$

where a and b are positive integers smaller than N. Because a and b are smaller than N, each can be factored as the product of primes, and hence their product, N, can also be written as a product of primes. This is a contradiction.

Uniqueness. Again I proceed by contradiction. Assume that a certain integer N has two different factorizations,[2]

$$N = p_1 p_2 \cdots p_r \qquad\qquad (C)$$

and

$$N = q_1 q_2 \cdots q_r \qquad\qquad (D)$$

I can assume, without loss of generality, that N is the smallest such integer.

Now $p_i \neq q_j$ for $0 \leq i \leq r$ and $0 \leq j \leq s$, because if there were such a p_i and q_j, the integer $M = \frac{N}{p_i}$ would both be smaller than N and have two different factorizations. This is contrary to N being the smallest such integer with this property. Thus I can assume without loss of generality[3] that $p_1 < q_j, 0 \leq j \leq s$, and, keeping in mind that N is the least integer with two different factorizations, I have

$$q_1 = d \cdot p_1 + t$$

where $1 \leq d$ and $0 < t < p_1$. If I substitute this in (D), I have

$$N = (d \cdot p_1 + t) q_2 \cdots q_r$$
$$= d \cdot p_1 \cdot q_2 \cdots q_r + t \cdot q_2 \cdots q_r$$

Set

$$M = N - d \cdot p_1 \cdot q_2 \cdots q_r$$
$$= t \cdot q_2 \cdots q_r$$

Factoring out p_1 gives

$$M = p_1 \cdot (p_2 \cdots p_r - d \cdot q_2 \cdots q_r)$$

---

[1] The well-ordering principle states that every nonempty set of positive integers contains a smallest member.
[2] Note that a prime may be repeated in this factorization.
[3] Say, for example, I list the q_j in decreasing order and then compare the p_i to the least in that series. If one of the p_i is less than all the q_j, then I have finished. If none of the p_i is less than that least q_j, then I, in effect, interchange (C) and (D) in the proof.

Thus there is a prime factorization of M that includes p_1, but there is also one that does not:

$$M = t \cdot q_2 \cdots q_r$$

Because $1 \leq d$, I have $M < N$ and hence a contradiction, as N was the smallest integer with this property.

So, as was to be shown, every composite number N can be factored uniquely into prime factors:

$$N = p_1^{a_1} p_2^{a_2} \cdots p_r^{a_r}$$

where the p_i's are the various different prime factors and a_i is the multiplicity.

Index

A

abacus, 29
addends, 19
addition, 26–45
    arithmetic series and figurate numbers in, 37–41
    associative property of, 163
    commutative property of, 163
    of decimals, 122–123
    developmental perspective on, 29–31
    of fractions, 107–111
    historical perspective on, 26–29
    indeterminate problems in, 41–44
    of infinite numbers, 156
    of negative numbers, 59–60
    repeated, 70
    whole-number algorithms for, 32–37
additions algorithm for subtraction, 48, 50
additive cancellation, 163
additivity, in arithmetic of remainders, 92
Ahmes Papyrus, 81, 101
aleph-null ($\aleph_0$), as infinity representation, 151, 155–159
algorithms
    for addition, 32–37
    for division, 85, 87–89
    Euclid's, 106
    for fractions
        addition and subtraction of, 107–111
        multiplication and division of, 111–114
    for multiplication, 72–75
    for subtraction, 52–57
        decomposition, 53–55
        equal-additions, 55–56
        left-to-right, 56
        overview of, 48–50
        standard, 54, 57
al-Khowârizmi, 95
al-Kushi, 132

alternative addition algorithm, 34
apeiron (infinity), 148
apodeixis (Greek proof), 3, 6–7
approximation, 132
Archimedes, 41, 68, 131–132, 135
area, comparing, 2
Aristotle, 148
arithmetic
    clock, 21, 90–94
    decimals in, 122–125
    fractions in, 103–114
        addition and subtraction algorithms for, 107–111
        equivalent, 104–107
        multiplication and division algorithms for, 111–114
    Fundamental Theorem of Arithmetic for, 78, 142, 161, 163–165
    infinite numbers in, 156–159
    modular, 90–94
    properties of, 162–163
    real numbers in, 136–139
    of remainders, 91–93
    subtraction in, 46
Arithmetica (Diophantus), 57
arithmetic series, 37–41
Aryabhata, 131
associative property of addition, 163
associative property of multiplication, 163
Attic Greek numerals, 12

B

Base-6, subtraction in, 56–57
Base-10; *see also* decimals
    addition in, 32–36
    expanded notation in, 22
    subtraction in, 53–56
base-2, 36
Bháskara, 102
billion, 23

binary system, 21
blocks, unit, 1
borrowing, as subtraction algorithm, 48
Brahmagupta, 43, 58, 131
Brownell's modification, 48
building up strategy, 116

C

cancellation, additive and
    multiplicative, 163
Canto of Algorismo (de Villa Dei), 29
Cantor, George, 148, 151, 155
cardinality, 30, 151, 154
casting out nines method, 95–96
Chinese numeral system, 12
ciphered numeral systems, 13
circumference of circles, 131–132, 135
clay tablet, 26
clock arithmetic, 21, 90–94
coefficients, 43, 57
combination method, for
    multiplication, 70
combinatorics, 20
common denominators, of fractions, 109
common fractions, 102
commutative property of addition, 163
commutative property of
    multiplication, 71, 163
complex numbers, 129
computers, binary system for, 21
congruences, 2, 90–91, 94, 96
conjectures, 3, 8, 19
continued fractions, 143–144
contradiction, proof by, 8–10, 77, 130, 155
counting, 3, 11–25; *see also* addition
    combinatorics and, 20
    developmental perspective on, 14
    down, 50
    functions and, 17–19
    historical perspective on, 11–14
    infinity and, 148
    large numbers, 23–24
    positional number systems for, 21–23
    sets and, 15–16
covariation, 115
Craft of Nombrynge, The (Steele), 29
cross-multiplication, 116

D

decimals, 119–128; *see also* fractions
    addition and subtraction of, 122–123
    developmental perspective on, 120–122
    historical perspective on, 119–120
    multiplication and division of, 123–125
    nonrepeating nonterminating, 129, 143
    nonterminating, 125–126, 137–138
    notation for, 101
decomposition algorithm for subtraction
    in base 10, 53–55
    description of, 48–49
deduction, 3
de Muris, Johannis, 119
denominators, of fractions, 107, 109
de Villa Dei, Alexander, 29
differences; *see* subtraction
Diophantus, 57
displacement, on number line, 58
distributive property
    definition of, 163
    for functions, 19
    in multiplication, 72, 74
    in subtraction, 54–55, 57
dividends, 86
divisibility, 94–95
division, 81–99
    casting out nines method for, 95–96
    clock arithmetic and, 90–94
    of decimals, 123–125
    developmental perspective on, 85–87
    divisibility and, 94–95
    of fractions, 111–114
    historical perspective on, 81–85
    indeterminate problems in, 96–98
    of infinite numbers, 158–159
    whole-number algorithms for, 87–89
doubling numbers, 65–66
duplation (doubling), 66

E

Egyptian recording systems, 11–12
Elements (Euclid), 2–3, 106
equal-additions algorithm for subtraction,
    48–49, 55–56
equivalent fractions, 104–107, 124
Eratosthenes' sieve, 76
estimation, 34, 87
Euclid, 2–3, 76–77, 87, 106, 114, 163
Eutocius of Ascalon, 68
even numbers, 3, 6
exhaustion, proof by, 4–6
expanded notation, 21–22
exponents, 162

F

factoring, 62, 78–79, 163–165; *see also* prime numbers
Fa jing (Kui), 46
figurate numbers, 37–41
fractions, 100–118; *see also* decimals
  arithmetic with, 103–114
    addition and subtraction algorithms for, 107–111
    equivalent fractions in, 104–107
    multiplication and division algorithms for, 111–114
  continued, 143–144
  developmental perspective on, 102–103
  historical perspective on, 100–102
  ratios and proportionality with, 114–116
  rounding and, 66
functions, 17–19, 43
Fundamental Theorem of Arithmetic, 78, 142, 161, 163–165

G

galley method of division, 84
Gantia Sara-Sangraha (Mahaviracarya), 44
Garfield, James, 139
Gauss, Karl Friedrich, 38, 90, 148, 163
Gobar (dust) numerals, 13
Golden Ratio, 131, 144
greatest common divisors, of fractions, 110
Grounde of Artes, The (Recorde), 47, 85, 102
grouping systems, multiplicative, 12
guess and check methods, 42

H

halving, 66
Herodotus, 27
Hindu-Arabic numeral systems, 13
Holder's Arithmetic, 84
horizontal additive process, 34

I

imaginary numbers, 129
indeterminate problems
  in addition, 41–44
  in division, 96–98
induction, proof by, 7–8, 19, 38
infinite decimals, 119, 125–126
infinite numbers, 147–160
  addition and subtraction of, 156–157
  developmental perspective on, 149–151

historical perspective on, 147–148
multiplication and division of, 157–159
varieties of, 151–156
Introductio arithmetica (Nicomachus of Gerasa), 69
irrational numbers, 129, 143

J

Jains mathematicians, 147
Japanese numeral system, 12
Joseph, George C., 3

K

Kui, Li, 46

L

large numbers, 23–24
least common denominators, of fractions, 109
least common divisors, of fractions, 110
left-to-right algorithm for subtraction, 56
lemmas, 4
logical deduction, 3

M

Mahaviracarya, 44
making ten, 34
Measurement of the Circle, The (Archimedes), 68
mediation (halving), 66
memorizing multiplication tables, 70–71
minimal equivalent, in fraction reduction, 106
minuends, 54–55, 58
modular arithmetic, 90–94
Moser, Leo, 23–24
multiplication, 65–80
  associative property of, 163
  commutative property of, 163
  of decimals, 123–125
  developmental perspective on, 70–72
  factoring and, 78–79
  of fractions, 111–114
  historical perspective on, 65–70
  of infinite numbers, 157–158
  of negative numbers, 61–63
  prime numbers and, 75–77
  proportions and, 116
  whole-number algorithms for, 72–75
multiplicative cancellation, 163

multiplicative grouping systems, 12
multiplicativity, in arithmetic of
        remainders, 92–93

N

natural logarithms (*e*), 131
natural numbers; *see* real numbers
negative numbers, 57–63
    adding, 59–60
    multiplying, 61–63
    on number line, 57–59
    subtracting, 60–61
Nicomachus of Gerasa, 69
Nine Chapters on the Mathematical Art, The
        (Suanshu), 57
nonrepeating nonterminating decimals,
        129, 143
nonterminating decimals, 119, 125–126,
        137–138
notations
    decimal, 101
    expanded, 21–22
    functional, 43
    for set operations, 16
number line, 57–59, 104, 153

O

odd numbers, 3
ordering, total, 163
ordinality, 14

P

Pacioli, Luca, 69
pairs, groups of, 6
paradoxes of Zeno, 148
partitioning problems, fractions as, 103
patterns, systematic, 3, 5
Pellizzati, Francesco, 120
permutations, 20
Physics (Aristotle), 148
pi (∏), 131–132
polygonal numbers, 40
polygons, 132
positional number systems, 21–23
postulational proof, 6–7
potentially infinite numbers, 148
powers of 10, 54
Pratt-Cotter, Mary, 48
prime numbers, 8–10, 142, 163–165; *see*
        also factoring

Prime Number theorem, 77
products, 70, 111; *see also* multiplication
proof
    by contradiction, 8–10, 77, 130, 155
    developmental perspective on, 3
    by exhaustion, 4–6
    historical perspective on, 2–3
    by induction, 7–8, 19, 38
    postulational, 6–7
proportionality, 114–116
propositional logic, 3–4
Pythagorean Theorem, 2, 131, 135,
        139–143

Q

quotients, 86; *see also* division

R

rational numbers, 119; *see also* fractions
ration tablet, 26–27
ratios, 114–116
real numbers, 129–146
    arithmetic with, 136–139
    continued fractions in, 143–144
    developmental perspective on,
        135–136
    historical perspective on, 131–135
    overview of, 129–131
    Pythagorean Theorem and,
        139–143
reasoning, proportional, 115
reciprocals, of fractions, 114
Recorde, Robert, 47, 85, 102
rectangles, 2
reduction, in fraction arithmetic, 105
reflexivity, in arithmetic of remainders,
        91, 93
regrouping, 34
remainders, arithmetic of, 91–93; *see*
        also division
repeated addition, 70
representational systems, for
        counting, 11
Rhind Papyrus, 65, 81
Roman counting board, 27
Ross, Susan, 48
rote association, 71
rounding, 66
Rudolf, Christian, 120
Rule of Three, in proportions, 116

S

"scaffolding," in division, 87
scratch method of division, 82
separatrix (decimal point), 120
sequential order of numbers, 14
series, arithmetic, 37–41
sets, 15–16
sexagesimal fractions, 101, 119
sharing, division and, 85
sieve of Eratosthenes, 76
signed numbers, 57
simple grouping systems, 12
simultaneous equations, 57
skip-counting strategies, 70, 76
square root of 2, 132–135, 143
squares, 1, 135
standard addition algorithm, 34
standard division algorithm, 85
standard subtraction algorithm, 54, 57
Steele, Robert, 29
Stevin, Simon, 120–121
Suanshu, Jiuzhang, 57
subscripts, 162
subtraction, 42, 46–64
    of decimals, 122–123
    developmental perspective on, 49–52
    of fractions, 107–111
    historical perspective on, 46–49
    of infinite numbers, 156–157
    negative numbers and, 57–63
    whole-number algorithms for, 52–57
subtrahends, 54–55, 58
*Summa de arithmetica, geometrica,
        proportioni et proportionolita*
        (Pacioli), 69
sums; *see* addition
symbolic postulational proof, 6
symmetry, in arithmetic of remainders, 92

T

tabular approaches, 42
tagging schemes, 18
tally stick, 11
10; *see* base 10; decimals

Theon, 133
theorems, 2, 4
    Fundamental Theorem of Arithmetic,
        78, 142, 161, 163–165
    Prime Number theorem, 77
    Pythagorean Theorem, 131, 135,
        139–143
total ordering, 163
transfinite numbers; *see* infinite numbers
transitivity, in arithmetic of remainders,
        92–93
trial and error, 3
trial multipliers, 82
triangles, 1
2, square root of, 132–135, 143

U

unit blocks, 1
upapattis (Indian proof), 3

V

variables, 161–162
vector differences, 58
Vedic mathematicians, 147
Venn diagrams, 16
vulgar fractions, 102

W

whole-number algorithms; *see also*
        real numbers
    for addition, 32–37
    for division, 87–89
    for multiplication, 72–75
    for subtraction, 52–57
whole-number partitioning problems,
        fractions as, 103

Y

Yale Babylonian Collection, 26
YouTube, 69

Z

Zeno, paradoxes of, 148
zero, 21, 36, 59